born on the 8th

proseys (as in poems)

Nona Mock Wyman

Cover photo taken by Eastfield Ming Quong.

Graphic design: Pamela Wong

Special Thanks for Her Advice and Support –
Publisher: Donna Van Sant

For permission requests, write to the publisher, addressed "Attention: Permissions Coordinator," at the address below.

dvs Publishing
2824 Winthrop Ave.
San Ramon, CA 94583

Printed in the United States of America

ISBN 978-0-9977484-2-0

DEDICATION

TO MY WONDERFUL 'ONE-OF-A-KIND CUSTOMERS AND FRIENDS'
LEARNING FROM EACH OF YOU IN EVERYDAY ENCOUNTERS
WAS EDUCATIONAL AND LIFE FULL-FILLING
'THANK YOU'

FOR – JERRY BALL – SPECIAL – LOVING GRATITUDE
HIS GUIDANCE – HIS FRIENDSHIP INSURMOUNTABLE

LEGACY OF LOVE
GENEROSITY FOR ALL
UNEXPECTED WIT

NOTE: A HAIKU FOR JERRY'S PASSING

– 8/14/2019

Ming Quong celebrated its 50th year in October, 2019

1517 ½ N Main Street
Walnut Creek, California 94596 • Phone (925) 939-8346

TABLE OF CONTENTS

EXPLANATION
FOR
BORN ON THE 8ᵀᴴ

THIS UNEXPECTED TITLE
HAPPENED — BECAUSE OF MY MOTTO
"BE OPEN FOR THE UNEXPECTED"
DURING THE CHRISTMAS SEASON
THREE CHINESE PEOPLE IN THE STORE, FROM HAWAII
SURNAME — 'MOCK,' — JUST LIKE MINE!

A MARSHALL MOCK, HIS WIFE, AND SISTER
THE CHINESE CULTURE — ALL MOCKS ARE RELATED
DR. MOCK'S UNEXPECTED SHARING — "WE ARE FROM 'ROYALTY'!"
THEY PROMISED — 'THE MOCK GENEALOGY' – IT ARRIVED
ASTOUNDED — 'ROYALTY' — RIGHT BEFORE MY EYES!

FASCINATED, I EXPLORED THIS NEW PATHWAY COMPOSING THOUGHTS
WHICH LEAD TO — POEMS — BUT, WAS TOLD
SOME OF MY POEMS WERE LIKE PROSE
WHICH INSPIRED, MY NEW WORD: 'PROSEY'
WELCOME TO SOME 'PROSEY' POEMS!

Reflections:

In 2018, my mentor and friend, Jerry Ball had Parkinson, which made it difficult to understand his wise teachings. Grateful ever, as he taught me haiku, tanka & haibun, plus now: "long poems". Jerry with his infinite patience, listened, spoke words of encouragement, his wit beyond everyday thinking, always with it…

Notes on my 'new-found 'Mock' relatives': Marshall's wife snapped a photo of the '3 Mocks.' A treasured photo – Dr. Marshall Mock, PhD. Physics, retired from Kaua'i Community College, connected to the 'black hole' – sister, Michelle Mock Lindberg, of Oakland, Ca. sent the genealogy. The Mock picture is in the *Ten Thousand Flowers* book.

FACTS TO KNOW IN THIS BOOK

1. **MING QUONG HOME** — *A CHINESE GIRLS' ORPHANAGE LOCATED IN LOS GATOS & OAKLAND, CA, IN THE 1930'S.*

2. **MING QUONG** — *NAME OF THE STORE IN WALNUT CREEK, CA. DUBBED ONE OF THE '7 WONDERS OF THE EAST BAY' BY THE CONTRA COSTA TIMES. MQ STORE HAS BEEN IN EXISTENCE FOR 50 YEARS, AS OF OCTOBER 2019.*

3. **MING QUONG (明光)** — *MEANS 'RADIANT LIGHT', SPIRITUALLY IN CANTONESE. ACADEMICALLY IT MEANS, SMART, BRILLIANT, BRIGHT, OR SHINY.*

4. **UPLIFT FAMILY SERVICES** — *CURRENT HQ IN CAMPBELL, CA. ESTABLISHED IN 1867 AS EASTFIELD HOME OF BENEVOLENCE, IT WAS THE FIRST ORPHANAGE IN SAN JOSE. EASTFIELD MERGED IN 1987 WITH MING QUONG (EMQ), LATER TO BE CALLED, EMQ CHILDREN & FAMILY SERVICES.*

5. **CHUNG MEI** — *A BOYS' HOME LOCATED AT 1800 ELM STREET IN EL CERRITO, CA, IN THE 1930'S. A HISTORIC LANDMARK.*

6. **'920' ALSO KNOWN AS 'THE MISSION HOME'** — *FOUNDED IN 1874, AND LOCATED ON SACRAMENTO STREET IN SAN FRANCISCO, CHINATOWN, THIS ORGANIZATION RESCUED EXPLOITED CHINESE WOMEN. RENAMED 'CAMERON HOUSE', BY MARCH FONG EU, SECRETARY OF STATE. TODAY'S YOUTH FROM SF & BEYOND ENJOY THEIR DIVERSE ACTIVITIES. SAN FRANCISCO'S 44TH HISTORIC LANDMARK.*

7. **BOOKS BY THE AUTHOR** — *CHOPSTICK CHILDHOOD, BAMBOO WOMEN, and TEN THOUSAND FLOWERS.*

8. **4TH BOOK** — *BORN ON THE 8th* — *** CONTAINS 'PROSEY' POEMS ON VARIOUS SUBJECTS WHICH MOVED MY SOUL. BY COINCIDENCE, THERE ARE '50' POEMS, ONE FOR EACH YEAR MQ HAS BEEN IN BUSINESS! PLUS ONE TO GROW ON!!!

   'PROSEY' MEANS THE POEMS ARE MORE DESCRIPTIVE THAN A 'REGULAR' POEM!

   ***NOTE – THIS BOOK IN 'ALL CAPS' – ESPECIALLY FOR 'SENIOR EYES'!

PICTURES FROM THE POEMS

READ THE CORRESPONDING PROSEYS – PAGE NUMBERS LISTED NEAR EACH PHOTO

3

27

52

48

25

30

X

IN ANCIENT CHINA — FROM KEI-TO-MOCK

OVER 2,000 YEARS AGO, CHINA'S LONGEST CULTURAL DYNASTY
'CHOU,' – LASTED OVER 800 YEARS
'8' – THE AUSPICIOUS NUMBER INTENSIFIED WITH TWO ZEROS
CHINA'S SPIRITUAL CORE THREATENED BY WAR
WARRIOR WUHUNG, A FORTHRIGHT MAN FOUGHT FIERCELY
AGAINST THE EVIL FORCE, SHANG — THUS BECAME:
THE 'FIRST KING SUN' OF THE KEI VILLAGE

KEI VILLAGE OF 700 SOULS RENAMED — 'MOCK' — BY THE EMPEROR
CHINA'S RECORDS – REVEALED THE MOCKS AS OFFSPRINGS OF KING SUN
HEIR TO THE THRONE OF CHINA! A RAGS TO RICHES PARADOX!
ORPHAN TO ROYALTY
UNSOLICITED COMMENT ABOUT 'ROYALTY' – "AM NOT SURPRISED, I CAN TELL!"
"HOW?" – MING QUONG'S CHINA BORN TEACHER, A GENTLE SOUL,
EMPHASIZED; 'PEOPLE FROM NORTHERN CHINA, 'TALLER AND REFINED'
OLDER SISTER, TALL WITH AN ELITIST ATTITUDE, – ME, TALL, AND EARTHY

CHOU DYNASTY HAD MANY PHILOSOPHERS, AS IN, CONFUCIUS – LAO TZU...
THIS DYNASTY WAS CHINA'S GEM, BANKS OVERFLOWED WITH ENRICHMENT
INHERENT – THEIR VERSATILITY – AN EVERYDAY UTENSIL CAME FORTH;
'CHOPSTICKS' – LIKE FUN PICK-UP STICKS, YET, SO PRACTICAL
ANCIENT MOCK VILLAGERS – POLITICALLY MINDED – JUDGES – HIGH OFFICES
INFLUENTIAL WITH THE JUDICIAL SYSTEM
MOCK CHAI, AN OFFICIAL, PUBLISHED HIS POETRY BOOK
MY 'INHERITED' TRAIT?

A NON-COMPUTER PERSON – YET – SEARCHED WEBSITES
ABSORBED HISTORY BEYOND THE REALM OF REALITY
MARCO POLO'S DISCOVERY OF CHINA — MY EDUCATION IN DISCOVERIES
A TRINITY OF KNOWLEDGE
THE 'CHOU DYNASTY' – THE 'KIE VILLAGE' – THE 'MOCK VILLAGE'
FROM 'NORTHERN CHINA' CAME – 'MOCK CHAI'

2,000 YEARS LATER
FROM 'NORTHERN 'CALIFORNIA' CAME – 'NONA MOCK'
PUBLISHED – BOOK OF POEMS
MY – 'INHERITED TRAIT'

Facts:

Records at the Ancestral Hall, Sun Wah District, Kwongtung Providence, China.

Chou Dynasty also known as the Zhou Dynasty.
(Poem - 8/1/2018 - printed 2019.)

A DIFFERENT PLACE — A DIFFERENT TIME

IN A WORLD WHERE NO ONE KNOWS WHAT HAPPENS NEXT
I WAS INVITED TO SHARE MY BOOK, *CHOPSTICK CHILDHOOD*
AND TO DINE WITH A LOCAL BOOK CLUB GROUP

I HESITATED RECOVERING FROM A 'KNEE-REPLACEMENT'
TIRED WAS I – BUT PLEASED
HER ENTHUSIASM MOUNTED

HOW COULD I REFUSE A SINCERE VOICE COMPLIMENTING ME?

THEN I RECALLED A COMMITMENT TO MYSELF
TO ALWAYS SHARE MY ORPHANAGE UPBRINGING
'YES' – I SMILED – HER JOYFUL SIGH CAME THROUGH THE PHONE

WE DINED, CHATTED AS MY STORY UNFOLDED:

AS A TWO YEAR OLD MY MOTHER ABANDONED ME
VOID OF EXPRESSION SHE WALKED OUT THE DOOR
LEFT ME SCREAMING IN THE ARMS OF A STRANGER

WHY? – I NOW ASK... – AN EMERGENCY?
SHE KEPT A STALWART FRONT — WHY?
SO HER YOUNGEST DAUGHTER COULD BE BRAVER?

THIS NEW LIFE, EMBRACED ME FULLY
MY LONELINESS EASED BY MY ACCEPTANCE OF NEW FRIENDS
WHO IN THEIR OWN WAYS 'MOTHERED' ME

THE LINGERING QUESTION – WHAT BECAME OF MY MOTHER?
THAT DAY – SHE GAVE UP HER YOUNGEST CHILD
MEMORIES OF HER – ARE HEARTWARMING
A SHORT LIFE TOGETHER – MADE BEARABLE BY THE LOVE WE SHARED...

THIS BOOK GROUP – WITH THEIR EARS TO HEAR –
ADJUSTING – ASSIMILATING
NOW ASCERTAIN WHAT LIFE WAS LIKE IN
A DIFFERENT PLACE – A DIFFERENT TIME...

FOR THE WALNUT CREEK BOOK GROUP MARCH 26, 2018

Reflections:

At Christine Odegard Donohoe's 'welcoming' home, this Walnut Creek
book-of-the month club opened new thoughts of my mother, hence –
this 1st poem – followed by more poems, which birthed into – *Born on the 8th*:
my 1st book of long poems.

THE SECRETARY OF STATE

FOR MY TINY RETAIL STORE — MING QUONG
I HAVE 3 SECRETARIES — ME, MYSELF AND I
'4' ACTUALLY! I FORGOT — THE SECRETARY OF STATE OF CALIFORNIA!
YES, 'THE' SECRETARY! — THIS WOMAN WHO STOOD UP FOR WOMEN'S RIGHT,
WAY BACK WHEN — WOMEN PAID TEN CENTS TO PEE, — MEN, NOTHING!
THEREFORE — SHE CHANGED THE LAW!
THAT WAS — MARCH FONG — A MINORITY WOMAN IN OFFICE

THE FABLE OF MY 4TH SECRETARY, IS ALMOST TRUE!
AS SHE SURPRISED ME ONCE - 'BIG TIME' - MADE ME THINK,
"WHAT A SECRETARY!"
BUT, BEFORE THAT 'SURPRISE,' AN ENCOUNTER WITH 'THE SECRETARY'
YEARS BEFORE - AT THE SAN JOSE HISTORICAL PARK MUSEUM
MARCH ENDORSED *CHOPSTICK CHILDHOOD* - MY FIRST BOOK
OGLING HER STATURE, MY EYES NOTICED HER 'WINGED PIN'
WITH NARY A WORD, SHE GAVE ME HER COMPLIMENTARY AIRLINE PIN!
I HAD WINGED IT - ENDORSEMENT AND ALL!

WHEN *CHOPSTICK CHILDHOOD* WAS PUBLISHED, MARCH FONG (EU) WAS
THE AMBASSADOR FOR MICRONESIA - APPOINTED BY PRESIDENT BILL CLINTON
IMPRESSED - I USED HER NEW TITLE - REGRETTABLE! - NAIVENESS
FOR SHE HAD SET THE RECORD IN CALIFORNIA
AS THE 'FIRST CHINESE WOMAN' - TO BE OUR SECRETARY

WHAT FOLLOWED - AN UNFORGETTABLE - SECRETARIAL ACT
ON MY 60TH BIRTHDAY, - A DIFFERENT ENVELOPE,
WITH THE SEAL OF CALIFORNIA
INSIDE, AN OFFICIAL CALIFORNIA DOCUMENT —
TITLED: 'NONA HARKEN DAY'
"INVITING ALL CALIFORNIANS TO CELEBRATE MY BIRTHDAY" — (unbelievable!)
HOW COULD A CHINESE WOMAN WING A GIFT LIKE THAT? WITH POWER & DIGNITY
UNAFRAID TO BASH A TOILET IN PUBLIC! — — — (she actually broke the toilet!)
THAT WAS MARCH, — MY 'SECRETARY OF STATE'!

2018

Reflections:

Perhaps, when the Contra Costa's 'Women March' march annually,
they will know that over (50 years ago) this forward woman paved the way for
them to march independently free! Perhaps, a 'chant' or a 2nd slogan? We
'MARCH FREE!' — In 2018 – a 'new' printing for *Chopstick Childhood*.
I was able to change March's title to: 'Secretary of State' and add: 'CC' won an
award for 'Humanitarianism', for 'Woman of Distinction,' from the Soroptimist
International of the Americas. The late, March Fong Eu (March 29, 1922 –
December 21, 2017), was unaware of these changes…knowing her spirit, I
sensed her approval for projecting all women in another light.

EXCLUSION BECAME AN ACT OF...

ONLY 150 CHINESE ADMITTED DURING THE EXCLUSION ACT
WHY SO FEW? — CHINESE FEARED — HARD WORKERS WERE THEY
MANY HIRED FOR AMERICAN JOBS, JEALOUSY SURFACED
LABORING JOBS SLOUGHED OFF TO THE 'HEATHENS'

THE CHINESE — LABORED ON
BENEFITTING THEIR HOMELAND
WHERE CUSTOMS RULED LIKE A WARRIOR KING

IN THE WILD WEST — GREED, GUNS, TEMPERS RULED
PISTOL-PACKING COWBOYS BENT ON REVENGE
STOLE FROM THE 'CHINKS', CLAIMING ALL THEIR OWN
SOME MURDERED, CHINESE HAD NO RIGHTS...
YET, THEIR BACKBONE WAS NOT 'YELLOW!'

THE CHINESE EXCLUDED BECAME A MECCA
WOMEN EXPLODED WITH CHILDREN
SIX, TWELVE CHILDREN OR MORE
CHINATOWN'S POPULATION SWELLED

TEACHERS AMAZED AT THESE IDEAL STUDENTS
DEDICATED STUDIES FORGED THEM AHEAD

FOR THE PARENTS; — THIS EXCLUSION BECAME AN ACT OF THE UNEXPECTED
FOR THE CHILDREN; — IT BECAME AN INCLUSIVE ACT:
AMERICAN BORN CHILDREN.

THE CHILDREN'S INNOCENCE

OVER 135 YEARS AGO, HEADLINES SPLASHED
ACROSS THE COUNTRY
EXCLUSION, EXCLUSION, — 'KEEP THE CHINESE OUT'
DISCRIMINATION SIGNS DEPICTED CARICATURES
OF SLANTED EYES, YANKED PIGTAILS, STRANGE ATTIRE
THE WILD WEST DEEMED 'CHINKS' UNDESIRABLES —
PLUS THEY TOOK THEIR JOBS!

Harper's Weekly, 7 August 1869

ORPHANAGE LIVING KEPT US IN OUR OWN WORLD,
RACISTS' SLANGS, POSTERS — OBSERVED IN ADULTHOOD
WHITE MISSIONARY WOMEN OF THE PRESBYTERIAN FAITH
KEPT US SECURE, NAIVE

THE FESTIVE ANNUAL PARADE THROUGH OLD TOWN LOS GATOS
FEATURED US PROUD GIRLS DRESSED IN TRADITIONAL CHINESE GARB
AN OLDER GIRL, MIMICKED A WEARY FARMER, DONNED A COOLIE HAT
SHOULDERED A BAMBOO POLE, WITH BASKETS OF VEGETABLES AT EACH END

THIS VENDOR'S ACT, ALTHOUGH A CROWD PLEASER WAS AGAINST THE LAW!
THE 'CHINESE EXCLUSION ACT' HAD RULED — 'THE POLE', ILLEGAL
THE IMMIGRANTS' ONLY MEANS OF TRANSPORTATION!
ANGUISHED FATHERS — HUNGRY FAMILIES
WE WERE INNOCENT OF SUCH A BIAS LAW — ALSO, UNBEKNOWNST TO US
CHINESE WOMEN CONSIDERED WORTHLESS, LIKE BROKEN CHINA
WOMEN BECAME HOUSEHOLD DRUDGES
OTHERS LABELED — PROSTITUTES — PORTRAYED IN STEREOTYPE MOVIES
RUMORED: THESE KINDS OF WOMEN LIVED AT MING QUONG!

THE UNSPOKEN OATH BY THE CHURCH-GOING TEACHERS WAS:
'ALWAYS PROTECT THE INNOCENT GIRLS,
TOO YOUNG TO COMPREHEND SUCH FACTS'
GIRLS WONDERED, WHY THE TEACHERS, TURNED A DEAF EAR — WHEN ASKED
PERTINENT QUESTIONS — HISTORY, NOW DIGESTED!

TODAY'S MING QUONG WOMEN HAVE MET WITH UPLIFT FAMILY SERVICES,
A STATEWIDE NON-PROFIT ORGANIZATION,
TO CORRECT MISINFORMATION ON BROCHURES
WEBSITES WILL IDENTIFY THE 'MING QUONG HOME'
AS A HAVEN FOR NEEDY CHILDREN
A RELEASE TO THE PRESS —
A CORRECTION FOR THE LOS GATOS (NUMU) MUSEUM
INFORM COLLEGE PROFESSORS IN ASIAN STUDIES, THE CORRECTED FACTS

PRESERVING CALIFORNIA'S CHINESE HISTORY IMMORTALIZED
THE EXCLUSION ACT DERIDED THE CHINESE, YET, TODAY'S, CHINESE WOMEN
VOICED THEIR OBJECTIONS — AND CLARIFIED THE MING QUONG LEGACY...

8/17/2018

A HUNDRED YEAR OLD LEDGER

A HUNDRED NAMES OF NEEDY CHINESE GIRLS AND ORPHANS
FOUND IN MING QUONG'S HISTORIC LEDGER, DISCOVERED IN A CLOSET
AT THE FORMER MQ GIRL'S HOME, IN LOS GATOS, CALIFORNIA
1ST ENTRY – 1915 – GIRL FROM AFAR – ACROSS THE OCEAN – 'CHINA!'
THIS TREASURE – A MODERN FIND
AT LONG LAST – OUR OWN STORY REVEALED, BUT DISAPPOINTMENT SET IN
NO DEFINING WORDS! SIMPLY; 'UNFIT HOME!'
YET, EXCITEMENT FELT, AS OUR ENTRY – VALIDATED OUR BEING!
TO FIND A PERSON – STATE APPROXIMATE YEAR AND LIKE A SUSPENDED
MOMENT IN TIME – HISTORY WILL APPEAR! – FOR VICKI, THIS HAPPENED
VICKI — WHOSE MOTHER WORKED — LIVED AT MQ FOR FOUR SUMMERS,
TODAY. SHE FOUND HER MOTHER'S ENTRY, PLUS HER OWN ENTRY
BACK THEN RAISED, 'IN A TOWN OF SILVER SPOONS' WE RECALLED
VICKI AS THE GIRL, WHO HAD A RELATIVE WHO WAS A 'MOVIE-STAR!'
STARRY-EYED, WE OGLED HER IN WONDER AS WE RECALLED
MOVIES LIKE – *BAMBI* AND *SNOW WHITE* — BUT IMAGINE A REAL MOVIE STAR ON
A GIANT SCREEN AT A FANCY THEATER! — VICKI WAS NAMED AFTER HER UNCLE
'VICTOR' – HE ONCE PORTRAYED 'HOP SING' IN THE POPULAR *BONANZA* SERIES
ASTONISHED, BEYOND WORDS, TO DISCOVER THAT THIS SENIOR MING QUONG
WOMAN WAS AMONGST US TODAY, EXHILARATED, I EXCLAIMED, "OH, YOU'RE
'THE' VICKI" – REUNITED, AT THIS SIGNIFICANT, MING QUONG/UPLIFT FAMILY
SERVICES FIRST MEETING – AND, TO HAVE HER DISCOVER THE TWO NAMES
IN THE OLD LEDGER
MY HANDS CLAPPED SPONTANEOUSLY LIKE A CHILD
THE 'EARLY' ENTRIES FROM THE EARNEST RECORDER — NEATLY WRITTEN
AS YEARS PASSED, SOME SPACES LEFT BLANK, YOUNGER ENTRIES NOT SHOWN
TOO MANY NAMES?
PERHAPS UPDATED METHODS RECORDED NAMES DIFFERENTLY

LYNETTE PACKED THIS HEAVY KEEPSAKE FROM SEAL BEACH TO WALNUT CREEK
QUITE A FEAT FOR A PETITE WOMAN WHO RECENTLY CELEBRATED HER BIG 8-OH!
SHE JOYOUSLY REPEATED – "I KNEW THERE WAS A 'REASON' TO BRING THE
LEDGER." – PERFECT, AS 'UPLIFT' PEOPLE ALSO OBSERVED, 'A SPECIAL MOMENT!'

THE MEETING: 'TO CORRECT UPLIFT'S DATES, WORDS, AND INHABITANTS OF MQ'
TODAY WE, 'BAMBOO WOMEN,' ARE FOREVER PROUD, AS MING QUONG'S
SPIRITUAL MEANING — 'RADIANT LIGHT' WILL CONTINUE TO SHINE BRIGHTLY...

October 2018

Reflections:

Historic meeting: 10/25/18 in Walnut Creek, CA @ Modern China Cafe – with
Ming Quong's Elena Wong Viscovich, Janet Chang, Lynette Choy Gin, Sylvia
Lew, Nona Mock Wyman, Vicki & Alex Demasi – with Uplift Family Services'
representatives: Lisa Algeria & Kristin Cameron.

Uplift Family Services 🐦

Back Row (left to right): Janet Chang, Vicki Lee Demasi,
Elena Wong, Lynette Choy Gin, and Sylvia Lew

Front Row: Nona Mock Wyman

Photo by Kristin Cameron

Name	Age	Legal Residence	Placed By
152. Lee, Florence	7	Oakland, Cali.	Father
153. Wade, Gloria		San Francisco	Mother
154. Lee, Betty		San Francisco	Mother & Father
➡ 155. Mock, Nona	3	Menlo Park, Cali.	Santa Clara Co. Welfare
156. Wong, Nellie	15	Ogden, Utah	Juvenile Ct. Ogden
306. WONG, PATRICIA MAY		San Francisco	Parents
➡ 307. Lee, Vickie		San Francisco	Mother
308. Woo, AGNES		San Francisco	Mother

This ancient ledger is about four times larger than the partial section shown
above. The first entry was recorded in 1915 of a woman from China.

PASSING OF A MENTOR

NO SHOUTS FROM THE ROOFTOPS, 'RICHARD NELSON BOLLES DEAD AT AGE 90!'
THE LITERARY ICON OF OUR TIME, YET NOTHING IN THE LOCAL, NATIONAL NEWS
DID HE LIVE IN VAIN?

AT THE PEARLY GATES: THEIR RESPONSE, "SORRY, NEXT IN LINE!"
"BUT" — I HUMBLY ASK, "DID I NOT HELP MILLIONS FIND JOBS?
MY BOOK WAS A BEST-SELLER, I WAS REVERED!"

NO MATTER, A FORMER EPISCOPALIAN PRIEST, MARRIED NOT ONCE
BUT, FOUR TIMES — 1ST TIME – OVERLOOKED
AND HEAVEN ONLY KNOWS, EVEN THE 2ND AND 3RD MARRIAGES, YOU PASSED!
BUT THIS 4TH MARRIAGE BARRED YOU FROM THE CHURCH
IN ALL INNOCENCE, IT WAS – 'EAST MEETS WEST' – SHE, BEING ASIAN
YOU LISTENED TO YOUR HEART – "THIS WOMAN LOVED ME, SHE CARED FOR ME"
THIS FILIPINO WOMAN HAD THE SMARTS
A WORLDLY STORY, HOW YOU TWO MET
A NORDSTROM SALES LADY, SHE ENTICED YOU TO PURCHASE THE MOST
EXPENSIVE WATCH TO REAP A HIGHER RETURN ON HER PAYCHECK!
ON EARTH, AS YOU WILL KNOW — THERE ARE — CRAZY RICH ASIANS!
YOU SMILED, YOU KNEW – SHE WOULD LOVE AND CARE FOR YOU
SEVERAL TIMES — SHE SAVED YOUR LIFE...

YOU WERE A DETERMINED MAN WHO KNEW AND SPOKE YOUR MIND...
YOU HAVE NOW ASCENDED — "WELCOME"
TAKE HEED — UP HERE — RULES ARE NOT TO BE BROKEN

MAY YOU CONTEMPLATE THE *GOOD* WROUGHT BY YOUR BOOK
YOUR TALENT WAS UTILIZED WITH HUMILITY

YOU WENT ALONG WITH THE TIMES
YOU PERFORMED WELL — REST IN PEACE, FOR HEAVEN ONLY KNOWS
WHAT YOUR NEXT MISSION WILL BE...

August 2018

Polaroid photo by Nona

Reflections:

Dick's bestseller book, *What Color is your Parachute?* (for job-seekers) sold over ten million copies, encompassing foreign countries and different languages. I was interviewed by the 'Walnut Creek Historical Society.' Dick's suite of offices were above our store, formerly the old Walnut Creek Hotel; our store was the lobby. Dick endorsed *Ten Thousand Flowers*; "My experiences at the Ming Quong store." His heartfelt words, as only he could express, touched my soul. A memorable mentor, for me, and for millions!

NEW EMPLOYEE

TRAINING DAY – NEW GIRL EMPLOYEE FOR JIM
GREET THE FRIENDLY, BLOND, CAUCASIAN GIRL
WRONG!! CORRECTION – IT'S A GUY – NAMED WALLACE
OOPS, I KNOW I HEARD RIGHT, 'HER' FRIEND HAD TOLD ME

FEW DAYS PASSED — ANOTHER NEW EMPLOYEE?
NO, — — ITS WALLACE, TRANSFORMED: — WITH BLACK HAIR
HUH? NOW HE LOOKED ASIAN

ASKED ABOUT WALLACE'S DRAMATIC CHANGE
ANSWER: WALLACE IS CHINESE
PLUS HE IS A TRANSGENDER – A 1ST FOR ME

DAYS PASS, I CALL OUT OCCASIONALLY TO THE NEW WORKER
BUT THE NAME ESCAPES ME
SO I SAY, "UM UM," WAITING FOR THE FOG TO CLEAR

'UM UM' RESPONDS QUICKLY, SO QUICKLY, I SMILE BRIGHTLY
A-HA, THAT'S YOUR NEW NAME
SO IN A FORGETFUL MOMENT, I BEGIN AGAIN – 'UM UM'
NO MATTER WHAT — MAKES NO DIFFERENCE
WALLACE IS WALLACE – A GOOD ONE – WE ARE BLESSED...

Summer of 2018

9

A VOICE AND POEM LOVELY AS A TREE

AN EUPHORIC MAN WALKED INTO THE STORE
LIKE A GOD IN A WHITE FLOWING GARMENT
PEACE FOLLOWED HIS STRIDE

MULTITALENTED MAN WAS HE;
FORMER FOOTBALL STAR, ACTOR, MODEL
HIS PERSONA WAS FELT

HE HAD PERFORMED AT A RELATIVE'S MEMORIAL SERVICE
SANG SOLO, ACCOMPANIED BY HIS OWN GUITAR
TODAY'S KNOWLEDGE CAUGHT ME WIDE-EYED, NOW, HE WAS ALSO MUSICAL!

JOYFULLY, I ENTICED HIM TO SING
AND LIKE A SINGING BOWL, HIS VOICE SWELLED
TILL IT ENVELOPED THE STORE

THE SONG, OF HIS CHOICE:
"I THINK THAT I SHOULD NEVER SEE A POEM LOVELY AS A TREE…"
MY SENSES DRIFTED UPWARDS
RISING LIKE A HOST OF ACAPELLA SINGERS!

MY CONSCIOUSNESS REALIZED HIS SPIRITUAL NAME:
'RAM DASS', AS HIS GURU HAD NAMED HIM.
PERFECT — ALWAYS CONSCIOUS – GRACIOUS – ATTENTIVE

RAM WAS OUR REP — REPRESENTING SPIRITUAL GIFTS FOR THE SOUL
MY PRACTICE OF BEING 'OPEN TO UNEXPECTED WONDERS'
HAD JUST HAPPENED;
A VOICE, A POEM AND RAM DASS SINGING
LIKE THE TRINITY — IT WAS COMPLETE

August 17, 2018

Reflections:

Robert Ram Smith's CD: *Flame of Spirit* (Classic Songs of Ananda) available
@ the MQ store.

CHILD IN A SMALL ROOM

AS A MERE CHILD – I SAT ALONE IN A SMALL ROOM
BEFORE ME WAS A CLOSED DOOR
TO MY RIGHT – AN OPENED WINDOW WITH A WISPY CURTAIN
IT BLEW GENTLY BACK AND FORTH
ENTRANCED – WAS I

THAT DAY – I WAS AT THE 'MISSION'
KNOWN AS – '920' – ON SACRAMENTO STREET
ATOP SAN FRANCISCO'S CHINATOWN

WHY WAS I THERE? – MAYBE, AS A PRESCHOOLER
I WENT FOR A RIDE WITH MISS REBER AND MISS CHEW
MISS REBER WAS THE DRIVER OF THE HOME'S STATION WAGON

THEY COULD HAVE ATTENDED A MEETING WITH
DONALDINA CAMERON, KNOWN AS – 'THE ANGEL OF CHINATOWN'
THESE TWO TEACHERS ALWAYS FELT HER PRESENCE
AFTER THEIR VISITS TO THE MISSION
THEY WERE JOYFUL, LIKE BIRDS WITH A LILTING MELODY

THAT QUIET MORNING – NO 'ANGEL' APPEARED BEFORE ME
DID I DOZE OFF AND MISS HER?
AS PEACEFULNESS WAS FELT IN THE ROOM

OVER EIGHT DECADES PAST
YET, THIS DREAM-LIKE EPISODE
REMAINS...

2018

Reflections:

'The 'Mission/920' - Donaldina Cameron, former
administrator of the Mission, in SF's Chinatown.

Miss Reber and Miss Chew were teachers from the
Ming Quong Home in Los Gatos, CA.

PERFECT DISGUISE

UNDERCOVER MAN — UNDERMINING WHOM?
WHOM DID HE WORK FOR? UNDERGROUND HUSTLERS?

A WHITE MAN DISGUISED AS A WINO
HUNG OUT IN SAN FRANCISCO'S CHINATOWN
AMONGST THE CHINESE MEN
HE EAVESDROPPED ON WHISPERED WORDS

HE CAUGHT THE LATEST SCOOP
A SHIP LOAD WAS DOCKING WITH 'GIRLS FROM CHINA'
LUCRATIVE MONEY FOR THE SINISTER CHINESE AND WHITE LEECHERS

THE WINO STRAIGHTENED UP, SCURRIED UP THE HILL
TO A - RESCUE MISSION

CHINATOWN SQUAD ALERTED
RAMMED INTO ACTION — SUCCESS

WHO WAS THIS MAN?
LIKE A DISCIPLE, HE WORKED FOR THE LORD ALMIGHTY
GLORIFYING HIS NAME

RAISED IN CHINA
HE WAS — THE PERFECT DISGUISE...

September 8, 2018

Reflections:

Dr. Charles R. Shepherd worked undercover for the SFPD & for Donaldina Cameron. He & Cameron were friends. She was the factor for him being in charge of the Chung Mei Home. Active with the Chinese Baptist Church in San Francisco's Chinatown...an author, The Chung Mei Story. Charles & first wife, adopted a girl & lived in China. After the death of his first wife, he returned to America, remarried, had a son & daughter, and lived in the Bay Area.

A TRUE SHEPHERD WAS HE

LIKE THE FAMOUS PAINTING OF A SHEPHERD RESCUING STRAYS
THIS MAN WAS FOR REAL
HIS REPUTATION BECAME KNOWN!

HATCHET MEN ON THE ALERT! — THIS MAN'S LIFE — IN DANGER
GUIDED BY THE LIGHT OF GOD — HE ELUDED THEM
AT NIGHT — SHADOWED SIDEWALKS — TABOO
WALKED THE MIDDLE OF WELL LIT STREETS

KNOWN AS: 'THE 'CAPTAIN' — HE COMMANDED RESPECT
A SUPERINTENDENT IN CHARGE OF 'CHUNG MEI'
A 'HOME' FOR DISADVANTAGED BOYS
A MAN OF GOD — A REVEREND

MORTGAGE DUE — BOYS LEARNED QUICKLY
MONEY NEEDED TO KEEP THE BOYS WELL SHELTERED
"YES, SIR!" — OBEYING CAPTAIN'S ORDERS

WOOD CHOPPED WITH EXACTING SPEED, SOLD DOOR-TO-DOOR
NO FALTERING ALLOWED — OR DIRE CONSEQUENCES!
ALL JOBS, WELL EXECUTED...

CAPTAIN UTILIZED THE BOYS' TALENTS
GARBED IN MILITARY STYLE UNIFORMS, EACH 'CADET' MARCHED IN SYNC
THEY BECAME PROFESSIONALS — SOUGHT AFTER ENTERTAINERS
MADAME CHIANG KAI-SHEK — WIFE OF CHINA'S LEADER — IMPRESSED

FROM BOYS TO ADULTHOOD — SOME HONORED THE CAPTAIN;
ON THEIR WEDDING DAY — HE WAS THEIR MINISTER...

COMMANDING — DETERMINED — STRICT — FAIR
A TRUE SHEPHERD WAS HE

September 10, 2018

Reflections:

Dr. Charles R. Shepherd, a native of England,
fluent in the Cantonese dialect.

A Doctor of Theology, minister for various
churches in San Francisco's Chinatown, and
'Captain' for the Salvation Army.

OLDEST CHUNG MEI BOY ALIVE!

A CHUNG MEI 'BOY' READ, *CHOPSTICK CHILDHOOD*,
HIS QUESTION, "WHO DO YOU THINK YOU ARE,
ON A SOAPBOX TALKING ABOUT MING QUONG?"
STARTLED WAS I! — WHO WAS THIS TOM CHAN? — FEISTY AS A PIT BULL!
WORTHY OF AN ANSWER? 'YES' — NO MATTER WHAT!
MANNERS TAUGHT AT THE MING QUONG HOME — I REPLIED POLITELY
AS A MOTTO IN MY MIND STRUMMED ——— "LET IT GO!"
MIRACLES OF MIRACLES — TOM ENDED UP BEING SMARTER THAN SMART!
WE BECAME FRIENDS! ANSWERED 'ALL' QUESTIONS — WITHOUT HESITATION!
HE WAS FULL OF IT! — CORRECT ANSWERS, THAT IS!
PERFECT FOR A CONTESTANT ON ANY MONEY MAKING TV QUIZ SHOW!
LUNCHED WITH HIM AND WIFE, HE WOLFED IT DOWN;
THEN DISAPPEARED, WITH HIS CAMERA, SNAPPING PICTURES OF THE STORE
LATER — A SURPRISE FOR ME! — A HUMOROUS ALBUM,
OF A MEDITATING BALD MAN IN A CAVE
GREAT SHOTS — GOOD PHOTOGRAPHER
IN YOUTH, A DRIFTER WAS HE — BUMMED AROUND WHILE HIS FATHER WAS
HARD AT WORK — A LIFE CHANGING DAY IN 1928, DR. CHARLES SHEPHERD IN
JUVENILE COURT — JUDGEMENT GRANTED, HE BECAME TOM'S,
'LEGAL GUARDIAN'
UNDER HIS SUPERVISION' — TOM, RESCUED FROM A TONG RECRUITER

ONCE, ON A GUEST PANEL WITH CM 'BOYS' AND MQ 'GIRLS,' WE WERE BATTLING
THE PROS AND CONS OF EACH 'HOME' — TOM, AT THE START, ME, AT THE END!
A VAST DIFFERENCE OF APPRECIATION ISSUED FROM ME
DID TOM'S PERSONA KEEP DR. SHEPHERD, THE STRICTEST
'BOSSMAN' AROUND? HE WAS CALLED — THE 'CAPTAIN'!
FUELED WITH ENERGY, TOM COULD NOT STOP MOVING — ON HIS WEDDING DAY
HE HAD A RUBBER BAND ON HIS WRIST, A REMINDER TO WED!
— IN TOM'S WORDS:
"AS A PAYBACK FOR BEING A CHUNG MEI BOY, UNDER CAPTAIN'S CARE"
DR. SHEPHERD PERFORMED THE CEREMONY IN THE CHUNG MEI CHAPEL

IN THE MOMENT PHOTOGRAPHS, WHERE THE ACTION WAS — THERE WAS TOM,
VOLUNTEERING 31 YEARS FOR: – ACC – NOW – ASIAN COMMUNITY SERVICES
FOR HIS 90TH BIRTHDAY, HE RECEIVED NO SHIRTS, NO NECKTIES — NOTHING?
A-HA !! — A GIFT BEFITTING A MAN OF HIS CALIBER — A MOTORCYCLE!
FROM WIFE, SANDRA AND THEIR THREE DAUGHTERS…
ON 4/15/ 2019, HE WAS '100'! — I YELLED — "HAPPY BIRTHDAY TOM,
THE OLDEST, CHUNG MEI BOY ALIVE — AND THE MOST FEISTY!"

Reflections:

'The Oldest CM Boy Alive,' was Tom's quote! – Tom's wedding picture with the CM chapel in the background...

THE LAST SUPPER

AN ADULT COURSE IN ICONIC ART
ART STUDENT MARVELED — 12 SIBLINGS IN MY FAMILY'!
RICH COLORS – DEPICTED THE MODERN – 'LAST SUPPER'

IN THE 'LAST SUPPER', JESUS OF NAZARETH DINED WITH
12 DISCIPLES AND PARTOOK OF WINE
ONE PLOTTED BETRAYAL

SOLDIERS ON A RAMPAGE, BARGED IN
JESUS DRAGGED AWAY LIKE AN ANIMAL
MADE TO HOIST A CROSS, FOUR TIMES HIS WEIGHT

NAILED TO THE CROSS ON CALVARY MOUNTAIN — CRUCIFIED
A CROWN OF THORNS THRUST UPON HIS HEAD

"FATHER, FORGIVE THEM, FOR THEY KNOW NOT WHAT THEY DO."
THIRST LIKE A MAGNIFIED DESERT CONSUMED HIS BODY

WHO WAS THIS MAN WHO HEALED THE SICK?
CARED FOR THE DOWNTRODDEN?
A CARPENTER WAS HE

KNOWN AS THE — 'SON OF GOD' – AND – 'KING OF THE JEWS'
MOTHER — ANGUISHED
ROAR OF THE CROWD DIMMED
DARKNESS BLACKENED THE SKY...

THE MODERN ART PROJECT COMPLETED
INSTRUCTOR STUDIED THE 13 FACES
APPROVED — WITH A NOD

— Composed for Vera's extended family...
2018

TWO AWAKENINGS

LIKE SONGS STUCK ON AN OLD PHONOGRAPH PLAYER
TWO JESUS SONGS KEPT RINGING IN MY HEAD
BOTH COMPLETELY DIFFERENT — ONE 'HEART BREAKING' — ONE 'ENDURING'
THESE HYMNS INDICATE THE SONG-WRITERS WITNESSED THE LIFE OF JESUS

WERE YOU THERE WHEN THEY CRUCIFIED MY LORD? — WERE YOU THERE?
(REPEAT)
(CHORUS) – OH — OH — OH — OH — SOMETIMES — IT CAUSES ME TO
TREMBLE, TREMBLE, TREMBLE
WERE YOU THERE WHEN THEY CRUCIFIED MY LORD?

WERE YOU THERE WHEN THEY NAILED HIM TO THE CROSS? — WERE YOU THERE?
(REPEAT)
(CHORUS) – OH — OH — OH — OH...
(ENDING) — WERE YOU THERE WHEN THEY NAILED HIM TO THE CROSS?
WERE YOU THERE?

THIS SONG SUNG SLOWLY IN AGONIZING TONES WITH EMPHASIS ON THE FOUR
'OH'S AND THE THREE 'TREMBLES' LEND SOULFUL CREDENCE

(2ND SONG)
LIVING FOR JESUS — A LIFE THAT IS TRUE
STRIVING TO PLEASE HIM IN ALL THAT I DO
YIELDING ALLEGIANCE, GLAD HEARTED AND FREE
THIS IS THE PATHWAY OF BLESSINGS FOR ME

OH JESUS, LORD AND SAVIOUR
I GIVE MY LIFE TO THEE
FOR THY IN THINE ATONEMENT — DIDST GIVE THYSELF FOR ME
I OWN NO OTHER MASTER, MY HEART SHALL BE THY THRONE
MY LIFE I GIVE, TRANSFERS TO THEE — OH CHRIST, FOR THEE ALONE

THESE WORDS, LIKE A HOLY OATH
THE WRITER'S DEDICATION IS AMAZING — WAY BEYOND ANY SAVIOUR!
AFTER COMPOSING MY POEM, 'THE LAST SUPPER' — LAMENTING SONGS
FREQUENTED MY MIND — AS IN ANGUISH CRIES THE NIGHT
AM LEARNING THAT HYMNS ARE AKIN TO POETRY, THE 2ND SONG RHYMES!
THE MELODY MOVES ME TO ANOTHER AWAKENING!
'OUR ERA IS DIFFERENT — BUT, REALLY — IS IT TRULY DIFFERENT?'
'DEFINITELY' — THERE IS NO 'JESUS!'

2018

Reflections:

The songwriters 'after' Jesus' time – amazing. "Were You There (When They Crucified My Lord)" was first printed in 1899. "Living for Jesus" was written in 1917. Love felt deeply within each soul.

HEAVENLY LOVE

PURE UNADULTERATED LOVE — IS IT KNOWN TO MAN?
A RELIGIOUS SONG SEEMS TO FIT THE OMINOUS QUESTION
PURE AND SIMPLE, LIKEN TO 'FIRST LOVE'
LIFTING YOU UPWARDS TOWARDS — HEAVENLY LOVE

— example —
I COME TO THE GARDEN ALONE
WHILE THE DEW IS STILL ON THE ROSES
AND THE VOICE I HEAR FALLING ON MY EARS
HIS VOICE TO ME IS CALLING

— chorus —
AND HE WALKS WITH ME AND HE TALKS WITH ME
AND HE TELLS ME I AM HIS OWN
AND THE JOY WE SHARE AS WE TARRY THERE
NONE OTHER HAS EVER KNOWN...

HE SPEAKS AND THE SOUND OF HIS VOICE IS SO SWEET
THE BIRDS HUSH THEIR SINGING AND THE MELODY THAT HE GAVE TO ME
WITHIN MY HEART IS RINGING

— chorus —

I'D STAY IN THE GARDEN WITH HIM, THOUGH THE NIGHT AROUND ME BE FALLING
BUT HE BIDS ME GO THROUGH A VOICE OF WOE
HIS VOICE TO ME IS CALLING

— chorus —

THE MAN IN THE GARDEN WAS — 'JESUS'
JESUS CLOSE TO 2,000 YEARS AGO
DOES A MAN LIKE JESUS EXIST?
DOES PURE UNADULTERATED LOVE EXIST?
HEAVENLY LOVE — SONGS FROM THE HEART — GIVES HOPE...

2018

Reflections:

Teachers @ the Ming Quong Home in Los Gatos, CA were Presbyterians.
It seems favorite hymns sung repeatedly – stayed within my soul.

— "They are eternal..." A quote from Chris Tomlin.

Have not heard his Christian songs, but his feelings convey my thoughts.

Realization – songs/poetry are interconnected ... MQH was sponsored by the
Occidental Board of Mission during California's Gold Rush era.

NOTHING ON MY MIND TODAY

A WEEK AFTER JULY 4TH
TUNED INTO A VIDEO, SENT BY COMPUTER, VIA A RETIRED TEACHER,
JOHN WAYNE'S '4TH OF JULY' TRIBUTE WITH OTHER CELEBRITIES IN HIS ERA

THOUGHT IT — 'WOULD TURN ME OFF'
INSTEAD IT — 'TURNED ME ON'
VOICES RICH IN HARMONY PAYING TRIBUTE BY SINGING
A STANZA EACH OF — 'GOD BLESS AMERICA'.

A SOLID, UNDERSTANDABLE SONG
NO ROCK AND ROLL
NO HIP HOP — NO JUMPING MUSIC — NO RAP
JUST GOOD-OLE-FASHIONED WORDS AND MELODY

WHAT A BLESSING
ALL I CAN SAY IS — "GOD BLESS AMERICA"
AND "GOD BLESS YOU!"
FOR WITHOUT YOU, THERE WOULD BE NO AMERICA!

MY GOODNESS — WITH NOTHING ON MY MIND
I HAD A LOT TO SAY — SAGENESS EXPLODED!

AND LEST I FORGET JOHN WAYNE — AND LEST I FORGET THE TEACHER
PLUS ALL THE SINGERS — I, TOO BLESS THEM...
AND ONE LAST — VERY IMPORTANT PERSON ON MY MIND — ME!
LEST — I FORGET — 'GOD BLESS ME!'

NOTHING MORE ON MY MIND TODAY...

July 2018

19

FIRST BOYFRIEND – MY PERFECT ROLE MODEL

CHINESE FRIEND RELATED, "BAD NEWS, YOUR FIRST BOYFRIEND DIED!"
FIRST BOYFRIEND? NEVER CATEGORIZED AS SUCH
ALTHOUGH — HE WAS A FIRST! — A CHINESE GUY, FROM CHINATOWN

SEVEN DECADES EARLIER, PUBERTY HAD SET IN
NO TALKS ABOUT BOYS AND SEX AT THE 'HOME'
NO ROLE MODELS
GRAMMAR SCHOOL, FLEETING CRUSHES
ON CUTE WHITE GUYS, IN A TOWN OF WELL-OFF ANGLO-SAXONS
THIS GUY — WORLDLY, IN A TOWN OF LOW-INCOME CHINESE IMMIGRANTS

1ST BOYFRIEND HUNG AROUND CHINATOWN AND EVEN SMOKED! — OUT OF
SCHOOL, BEST POOL PLAYER, EASY ON THE EYES, ALL AROUND COOLNESS
I – YOUNGER — HIM – OLDER — A RECIPE FOR DISASTER?
NO ROLE MODELS

RULE AT THE 'HOME'. TEACHER, MUST MEET BOY FOR PERMISSION TO DATE
ABATED SMOKING — APPROVED — SHARED A SOFT DRINK,
WE SMILED, HEARTS QUICKENED, FACES BLUSHED, 1ST LOVE —
BOTH BECAME SMITTEN

A WORLDLY MONEY TRANSACTION: BEYOND MY AGE
HE BOUGHT A CAR WITH AN OLDER WOMAN! — A GIRLFRIEND?
NEVER ASKED, LESSON IN LOVE FOR A NAIVE ME?
NO ROLE MODEL — TO ASK!
DECADES LATER, SCHOOL REUNION — NAMES ON PLACARD IDENTIFIED
1ST BOYFRIEND WITH WIFE FROM CHINATOWN DAYS
NO INSTANT RECOGNITION BETWEEN HIM AND I
PEPPERED HIM WITH MEMORIES
'WIFE' — "HE WON'T REMEMBER YOU — HAD TOO MANY GIRLFRIENDS."
IGNORED REMARK — HOW COULD HE FORGET? OUR LOVE WAS SPECIAL!
SUDDENLY, HIS FACE GLOWED — LIKE THE STAR OF BETHLEHEM
MY WISH CAME TRUE — HE REMEMBERED
SPLIT SECOND LATER — TOTAL BLACKOUT
EXPRESSION — DEADPAN — I FOLLOWED SUIT
LIKE A TRUSTING, SIMPLE CHILD;
MY FIRST LOVE WAS SIMPLE — MY FIRST LOVE WAS PURE
NO ROLE MODEL NEEDED — HE WAS, MY PERFECT ROLE MODEL!

Reflections:

A former MQ alumni at our table, "His actions were like that of a 'stroke victim'." Interesting, as he was my 1st encounter with 'stroke!'
Sadly, the perfect role model!

THE ART OF LIVING

THE ART OF LIVING
IS HAVING THINGS TO DO
YET NOT DOING THEM

LIKE THIS POEM WITH IN
KEEPS STRUMMING IN MY HEAD

FINGERS FLYING
THOUGHTS RACING
SCRIBBLED ON SCRATCH PAPER
MY EYES — BEHOLD
MY BRAIN — ABSORBS

OH, FOR THE PASSION WITHIN ME
UTILIZE IT
SHARE IT

ONCE AGAIN
A THOUGHT IS FORMING
A NEW BEGINNING
A NEW POEM

WHAT SHOULD I DO?
THE ANSWER IS WITHIN YOU
GO WITH YOUR HEART
TILL IT BIRTHS

IS THAT NOT THE KNOWINGNESS OF ALL
WHICH IS THE ART OF LIVING!

A PRIVATE SCHOOL

HIDDEN IN MONTANA — A PRIVATE SCHOOL
A SECRET KEPT FROM OTHERS
A BOARDING SCHOOL FOR BLACKFOOT INDIANS
NOT A PRIVATE SCHOOL — BUT AN ORPHANAGE!

'ORPHAN TRAIN' LANDED HER IN CALIFORNIA — IN SUBURBIA,
EICHLER'S, MODERN HOMES, PROGRESSIVE — 1ST TO ACCEPT ALL RACES
BORE — FIVE SONS, ONE DAUGHTER

AFTER HER DEATH — A SON PAID HER TRIBUTE ON — 'MOTHER'S DAY'
HE HONORED HER WITH A VISIT TO HER PRIVATE SCHOOL — SAW THE TRUTH
HIS MOTHER'S SECRET INTENSIFIED – HIS HEART WRENCHED

HE STROLLED THE GROUNDS
A MAN'S VOICE BROKE HIS REVERIE
"WHO ARE YOU — ARE YOU A NATIVE?"

THE SON FELT CAMARADERIE
NO ONE HAD EVER SPOKEN TO HIM IN SUCH A MANNER
HE FELT HIS ROOTS — THEY BECAME ONE

THE BLACKFOOT INDIAN MAN SPOKE, "BE PROUD OF YOUR HERITAGE,
GROW YOUR HAIR LONG" — RINGLETS COVERED THE SON'S HEAD
A PONYTAIL BECAME HIS NEW SELF
INSIDE, HE GLOWED — HIS MOTHER'S DEMONS VANISHED

THE MOTHER'S GOAL, TO HAVE HER CHILDREN FIT INTO SOCIETY
THE SOUL OF THIS MOTHER HAD PROVIDED — GUIDANCE —
HER OFFSPRINGS FLOURISHED

THROUGHOUT THE YEARS — PRIVILEGED TO WITNESS HER SON'S GROWTH
A PROUD INDIVIDUAL
OUR FRIENDSHIP WARMED MY HEART

CAN ONE SAY — IGNORANCE IS BLISS?
UNBEKNOWNST TO THE MOTHER, I, TOO, WAS AN ORPHAN
WHO ONCE PROVIDED 'CHILD CARE' FOR HER SON
HAD SHE KNOWN — WOULD SHE HAVE LEFT HIM?

Reflections:

– I sensed David's mother felt my home was a safe haven.

Can you find David?
He's the cutest one. ☺

22

CHILDHOOD MEMORY BECAME VISIBLE

NEARLY 200 RELATIVES INCARCERATED
AS A CHILD — LITTLE MT, GROWING UP
HEARD THESE UNSPEAKABLE ATROCITIES

IT AFFECTED THE MIND OF THIS ENCUMBERED SOUL
VANISHED LIVES GONE — FOREVER LOST
SEARING MEMORIES REPLAYED

HE SOUGHT FULFILLMENT
FROM HIS HEARTACHE
SACREDNESS CAME FORTH;
'LOVE' — UNADULTERATED

TWENTY-FIVE 'BIOLOGICAL' CHILDREN
EACH CHILD REPRESENTING
THEIR ANCESTORS

Dedicated to MT and his relatives – 2018

This space was wasted, so "waste not – want not" – I added this picture and prose

'TWAS 30 YEARS AGO
ON A WINTRY NIGHT
SANTA CLAUS' HELPERS
LEFT A SURPRISE FOR JIM!

Reflections:

Ming Quong shirts — designed by Les Ong — creative nephew, son of my oldest half sister — Nancy Ellen Ong.

SELF-PITY

NAIVENESS, FEAR OF THE UNKNOWN
KILLED HUNDREDS OF HARD-WORKING FEMALE WORKERS
I MOURNED

THE WORKERS HAD NO IDEA
THEY PROJECTED TERROR
AS THEY CONTINUED THEIR FRANTIC PACE

AWE-STRUCK BY THEIR WORK ETHIC
I WATCHED IN SILENCE
AS RUMORS BELIED MY MIND

THEN — REALITY HIT
THEY HAD TO GO OR MY 'FRIENDS' WOULD PERISH
AND — I, FEARFUL OF THEIR ATTACK — STAYED INSIDE!

STREAMS OF WATER HIT THEM
THEY DIED WITH SUCH FORCE
HUNDREDS OF HONEY BEES VANISHED — 'DEAD!'

AND I WAS LEFT TO MOURN, SELF-PITY CREPT IN
WHERE ONCE I HAD WATCHED FASCINATED
NOW THERE WAS SILENCE

WHAT COULD I HAVE DONE?
CALLED FOR HELP SOONER

LEARNING MORE ABOUT THESE HARD-WORKING FEMALES
MY WONDERS OF NATURE ENHANCED

THE OTHER 'FRIENDS' I SAVED WERE NEW SUCCULENTS AND FLOWERS
FEARS NOW DIMINISHED
AS MOTHER NATURE AWAKENED ME

MY SELF-PITY — PATHETIC — A LESSON LEARNED...

WHO WANTS TO BE A LANDLORD?

NEVER A THOUGHT OF BECOMING A LANDLORD
NOT WITH THIS, 'HOLE IN THE WALL' AS A COMPETITOR ONCE SNEERED
HIS MEANING, 'OUR SPACE — TOO CRAMPED FOR WORTHINESS!'

LIVING UPSTAIRS — DRUNKEN, ILLITERATE TENANTS
WHO USED THE OUTSIDE WALLS AS THEIR PRIVATE CHAMBER
WITH VOMIT BEING A COMMON THING
AND WHO KNEW — WHAT ELSE UPSTAIRS!
CURSING, DRUNKEN RENTERS, AT TIMES UNBEARABLE
WHO WOULD WANT TO BE A LANDLORD?
WHILE — DOWNSTAIRS — MING QUONG CUSTOMERS, CHEERFUL AND SUNNY
MADE IT ALL WORTHWHILE
THE HOTEL MANAGER — MR. KELLEY
DAPPER, LIKE A MAN FROM A PRESTIGIOUS SAN FRANCISCO HOTEL
SO UNLIKE HIS 'GUESTS' AS HE REFERRED TO THEM

NEW LANDLORDS BOUGHT THIS OLD HOTEL
BUILDING EMERGED FROM A LOW-INCOME ROOM TO TODAY'S
PRESENTATION, — ABLE TO CHARGE MORE WITH NEW INNUENDOS
MEASURING FROM THE OUTSIDE OF THE STRUCTURE AND OTHER
FACTS ADDED, RENT ZOOMED, LIKE DESERT TEMPERATURES
WALNUT CREEK WAS THE NEW DESTINATION!

NOW — PREMIUM SPACE — ONE NEW OWNER WISHING US OUT — WITH BRIBES
AS LOYAL CUSTOMERS, RALLIED TO OUR DEFENSE — "SAVE MING QUONG!"
SAVED WE WERE — A HALF A CENTURY COME AND GONE

WHO WOULD HAVE KNOWN — OLDEST STORE ON NORTH MAIN
NAMED, 'ONE-OF-THE-7-WONDERS-OF-THE-EAST BAY'
BY THE — CONTRA COSTA TIMES
INTERVIEWED BY THE WALNUT CREEK HISTORICAL SOCIETY
FOR THEIR QUARTERLY BROCHURE
MARK HARRIGAN POSTED THE WCHS ARTICLE ON HIS:
'680/24 CORRIDOR HISTORY' ON FACEBOOK WITH CLOSE TO 150 HITS!
WONDER WHAT IT WOULD HAVE BEEN LIKE TO BE A LANDLORD?

REFLECTIONS: OF A DIVIDED CREEK

GUSHING WATER DIVIDES A PLACE OF BEAUTY
A CREEK REFLECTING THE CLEAR BLUE SKY
THE HOMELESS RESIDES BY THE MEANDERING CREEK
THROUGH SLEETED RAINS, STORMY WINDS FREEZING NIGHTS
TILL CARING INDIVIDUALS ACTIVATED AN UNUSED BUILDING

SUBURBANITES, SNUG IN THEIR BEDS
PEERING OUT AS STORMY WEATHER RAGES
SOME WITH A VIEW OF THE CREEK

HOMELESS HOLED UP FOR THE NIGHT AT ABANDONED ARMORY
SIDE BY SIDE, ROWS OF COTS, SLEEP COMES QUICKLY
HUNGRY, SMELLY, BUT TONITE, WARM ABODE, ON THURSDAYS
CHURCH OPEN FOR FREE SHOWERS, CLOTHING, LUNCHES

SPRING ARRIVES AND ALL IS TAME
HOMELESS RETURN TO THE CREEK'S CLEAR WATER
TREES LADENED WITH AMPLE FRUIT
LAZING UNDER A SHADED OAK TREE
SATISFIED BURPS, LAUGHTER ABOUNDS

SUBURBANITES, LIKE YOUNGSTERS ON A TREASURE HUNT
TRIP INTO BOUTIQUES FOR SPRING ARRIVALS
LUNCHING ON SHADED PATIOS
TWITTERING LIKE SINGING BIRDS
THEIR EYE-CATCHING APPAREL LANDSCAPE THE SCENE

THE SPARKLING WATERS OF THE CREEK MEANDERS
TRICKLING HAPPILY — FREE FOR ALL
YET, DIVIDING THE HOMELESS AND THE SUBURBANITES
REFLECTING THE CLEAR BLUE SKY ABOVE

THE BRENDA BUN

YOU SEE THEM EVERYWHERE, BUNS — BUNS — BUNS — WHAT ARE THEY?
A NEW BREAKFAST TREAT OR A GOURMET SNACK?
NO — NOT EVEN CLOSE!
THESE BUNS ARE FASHIONABLE — A CIRCLE ATOP A WOMEN'S HEAD!
AN ANGEL'S HALO? — A BUDDHA'S CROWN? — NOT QUITE!
THIS FASHION IS A BUN! — IT'S NAMESAKE:
'BRENDA WONG AOKI'
AWARDED THE — #1 — ASIAN STORYTELLER/PERFORMER OF OUR TIME
BRENDA PERFORMS AND TELLS STORIES WITH HER — 'BUN'
THE BUN UNWOUND IS LUXURIOUSLY THICK, LONG HAIR BELOW HER WAIST
USED AS A PROP, WHIPPED AROUND LIKE A PRECISE HAND FAN
SNAP — SNAP — SWISH — SWISH — WITH BODY TWISTING
HIGH AND LOW — ADJUSTING TO ALL ANGLES, IT CAN BE UTILIZED AS A DRAPE
TO HIDE HER FACE!
WHEN HAIR IS THRUST BACK, HER EXPRESSION ELICITS AWE
AUDIENCE MESMERIZED — HER FAITHFUL BUN — AT HER COMMAND!
FOR OVER 60 YEARS, THE PERFORMER'S HAIR HAS BEEN HER PERSONA
WITH THE EVER-CHANGING TIMES
THE BUN CAN BE COLORED IN ELECTRIFYING HUES
TODAY — BUNS, BUNS, AND MORE BUNS ARE AROUND EACH BEND
YOUNG OR OLD — MAKES NO DIFFERENCE
BIG OR SMALL — MAKES NO DIFFERENCE
EACH 'BRENDA BUN' — A STORY IN ITSELF...

Reflections:

Brenda is the oldest daughter of a Ming Quong alumni, Bessie Wong-Lum Aoki.
Her siblings include 4 sisters and 1 brother. Brenda can be contacted at
First Voice, in San Francisco, CA.

www.firstvoice.org/brendawongaoki

THE KISS METHOD

WHEN AN URGENT THOUGHT APPEARS, I CAN'T STOP NOW
ESPECIALLY AT THIS TIME OF YEAR — FOR CHRISTMAS IS A COMING AND THE
ORDERS ARE COMING IN AND THE BOXES ARE A PILING UP

BUT — ANXIETY BUILDS INSIDE ME
MY THOUGHTS OVERTAKE ME — AS MY NEW VENUE: 'PROSEY POEMS'
REACTS DIFFERENTLY — UNLIKE PROSE OR HAIKU, IT'S MORE URGENT
OR COULD IT BE EXHILARATED AGE? — HMMM!
LEAVING NOTES HERE AND THERE
WATCHING THE WORDS UNFOLD — LIKE IN A HYPNOTIC STATE
IT'S BEGINNING, IT'S COMING — THE BIRTH OF WORDS — LIKE MAGIC

BUT THEN — MY EYES SURVEY THE BOXES FULL OF MERCHANDISE
WHICH COMES FIRST?
STORE? OR THIS NEW PASSION?

BY, NOW — MY BODY OVER TAKES ME AND CRIES OUT — "I'M EXHAUSTED!"
OH DEAR — JUST LET IT GO, I TELL MYSELF!
JUST DO A LITTLE HERE — A LITTLE THERE — IT WORKED — I'M SMILING!

SIMPLE IS — AS SIMPLE DOES — LIKE THE **KISS** METHOD;
'KEEP IT SIMPLE STUPID' — OR AS AN 'MQ' GENTLE SOUL IN HER 90'S
ONCE SAID: "HOW ABOUT THE WORD KEEP IT 'SWEET'?"
AHH, SWEET, JUST LIKE HER!

A TIME TO WORK — A TIME TO CREATE — A TIME TO REST
IT'S THAT SIMPLE — ALL I HAVE TO DO IS REMEMBER — 'KISS'
AND WHEN I DO, I AM FREE — FREE TO DO ALL THREE
MY THOUGHT CAPTURED? YES, THIS POEM!

NOW ONLY TWO MORE OF THE KISS TO DO!
THEN, I'M HOME — FREE
BEFORE ANOTHER THOUGHT TAKES OVER!

Reflections:

The sweet MQ alumni, who used the word, 'sweet' – was Helen Kee.
The oldest MQ gal during my time @ the Home. Her story is in the
Bamboo Women book.

THE BAMBOO SPIRIT

A WISE, CHINESE WOMAN AND I
ELABORATED ABOUT 'MY LOVE OF BAMBOO'
WHEN IN EARNEST TONES — SHE BEGAN:
"LET ME TELL YOU WHAT MY FATHER
ALWAYS REPEATED TO ME WHEN I WAS GROWING UP:
'A GOOD WOMAN IS LIKE BAMBOO
WHEN THE WIND BLOWS, IT BENDS
IT DOESN'T BREAK.'"
MY HEART RESPONDED INSTANTLY
MY LOVE OF BAMBOO — EXPLODED WILDLY — LIKE AN AWAKENING;
THE BAMBOO SPIRIT

THAT ANCIENT SAYING WAS IMBUED IN THE MING QUONG WOMEN
RAISED WITH YOUNG GIRLS FROM DARK HISTORIES
ABUSE — NEGLECT… AND WITNESSES TO DEATH…

WE ENDURED — — — LIKE WILD BAMBOO, GROWING BELOW OUR HILL
OUR BAMBOO SPIRIT FUELED WITH REGIMENTED CARE
NEVER WENT UNNOTICED — WE HAD EACH OTHER
FUN SECRETS SHARED — MANY FUTURE ENDEAVORS
IN ALL EARNESTNESS — VOWING LIFE'S FRIENDSHIPS
WE EMERGED SUCCESSFULLY, WITH:
THE BAMBOO SPIRIT
NOW — AT EACH OF MY BOOK-READINGS
THE 'BAMBOO METAPHOR' IS INCLUDED
THIS SAYING FOUND ITS WAY INTO THE LISTENERS' HEARTS
LIKE A WISDOM LIGHT TURNED ON
MY 2ND BOOK PAID TRIBUTE TO THE BAMBOO SAYING – TITLED:
BAMBOO WOMEN

Reflections:

Bamboo Women tells the stories of 21 Ming Quong Home women;
covering their lives before the Home, their stay, followed by life after the
Home – BW was featured @ St. Mary's College in Moraga, CA, especially for
the faculty for 'International Women's Day' – by Maureen Little, instructor for
the Women's Studies group. – The bamboo metaphor, by Marlene Hoy. Both of
these women were MQ store customers for decades!

CHINA SPOKE...

CHINA PARTNERED WITH UNITED STATES FOR RECYCLABES
PERFECT — MAJORITY OF TRASH TO A FRUGAL CONTINENT
WHO BARGAINS FRUITFULLY!

'CLEANLINESS IS NEXT TO GODLINESS'
AS THE SAYING GOES
AS WITH US

WE ENJOY LUXURIOUS SHOWERS, — BATHS
ENJOY LAWNS — FLOWERS — PARKS
ENJOY OLYMPIC-SIZE POOLS — SPAS...

LIFE IN THE 'OLD WAYS' GONE?
NO — BUT — CHINA SPOKE
RECENT FLYER SENT TO HOUSEHOLD:
'ALL TRASH MUST BE CLEAN OR SCRAPED — NO RESIDUE ABOUNDS'
WE LISTENED — WE WERE REMINDED
TO USE RECYCLED WATER TO CLEAN TRASH
TO USE RECYCLED WATER FOR OUTDOOR USE
TO MODIFY LIFESTYLE

TRASH WEEK — WE HONORED OUR PARTNER'S NEW RULE
OUR REALIZATION — CLEANLINESS — IN ALL WAYS
BENEFICIAL FOR ALL MANKIND
CHINA SPOKE — WE HEARD — WE LISTENED — I RESPONDED — DID YOU?

Reflections:

Recycles overload – Since this poem in 2018 – the facts are:

- China alone, cannot handle this massive undertaking

- A fact: China had their own inspectors in America here – checking our
  trash. The pile they wouldn't accept was sky-high! Vietnam &
  Cambodia are now receiving our recyclables! Africa next?

- On Facebook – alarming videos – showed beaches & streams of
  rushing, gushing waters overflowing with trash from all countries!

Unbelievable — we are all (so) interconnected. We must awaken!
We must listen! We must do our part!

WE WASTE NOT

FRUGAL, WAS THAT CHINA'S WAY?
THE CHINESE TEACHERS AT THE ORPHANAGE
TAUGHT US SAVING WAYS, THE IMPORTANT ONE WAS:
SELF-WORTH — FOR OUR FUTURE

GROWING UP — CLEANLINESS, A MUST
'HOME'S' RULE — NURSERY GIRLS
TWO TOGETHER, BATH WATER SHARED, WE PLAYED, WE SPLASHED,
LAUGHTER ABOUNDED — UNAWARE OF SAVING — YET
WE WASTE NOT

ALL FOODS EATEN
IF NOT — SIT, TILL FINISHED — PUNISHED — NO PLAYTIME — EARLY TO BED
BREAKFAST, EVEN SOMETIMES LATE FOR SCHOOL!
YET, WE WASTE NOT

DISLIKED A CERTAIN FOOD
DRUMMED INTO OUR PSYCHE
"THINK OF ALL THE STARVING CHILDREN IN THE WORLD"
WE SIGHED, "WOULD THEY LIKE LUMPY MUSH? OR SLIMY EGGPLANTS?"
WE WASTE NOT

GROWN-UP MQ WOMEN
ALWAYS FINISH ALL ON PLATE
LEFTOVERS IN RESTAURANTS, EVEN IF IT'S RICE
DOGGIE BAGS FOR US!
WE WASTE NOT

GOOD HABITS RULED OUR LIVES
THRIFTY CHINESE WOMEN — PASSED ON TO GENERATIONS
CHINA'S ANCIENT WAYS? — OR CHINESE ORPHANAGE WAYS?

NO MATTER — THE 'HOME' TAUGHT US WELL
SELF-WORTH WAS THEIR GOAL
ACCOMPLISHED — WELL DONE
WE WASTE NOT

RED STICKS!

IN MODERN TIMES –
A CHINESE WOMAN RAN A 'HIP' STORE
IN SUBURBIA USA.
RAISED IN A RELIGIOUS ORPHANAGE
HER LIFE'S EXPERIENCES – BELOW PAR!

WHILE ORDERING ESOTERIC GIFTS FOR HER STORE
SHE MUSED – 'FORTUNE-TELLING' STICKS
INTRIGUED…SHE ORDERED THE RED STICKS

'ORIGINAL SOURCE' GIFTED THE STICKS TO HER
HAPPY INDEED – THIS GRATEFUL WOMAN BECAME
WALNUT CREEK'S – CHINESE FORTUNE-TELLER!

FOR ONLY 1.00 DOLLAR – ONE COULD HAVE THEIR FORTUNE READ
AND EVEN INCLUDE – A WISH
INTRIGUED – THEY PICKED A RED, CHINESE NUMBERED STICK

SOME FACES PORTRAYED SKEPTICISM
A FEW CLOSED EYES FOR CONCENTRATION
OTHERS, OVERJOYED WITH JUST THE PERFECT WORDS
WISHES ALTHOUGH SOMETIMES DENIED – WAS ALRIGHT!

NEW RITUAL FORMED – SEEKERS RETURNED WITH OTHERS
FORTUNE TELLING STICKS – A NEW WAY OF LIFE

ANCIENT CHINESE CULTURE – WITH BLUNT WORDS IN RHYME
OFFERED INSIGHTS THAT MODERN TIMES COULD UTILIZE

NOW THIS FORTUNE TELLING WOMAN MADE WISER
SHE OBSERVED, LIFE'S MYSTERIES, THE DESIRES OF PEOPLE
ALL THIS MODERN LEARNING FOR ONLY $ 1.00 !

Facts:

Chinese Fortune Red Sticks is the world's oldest known method of fortune telling.

The 'reading' comes from a booklet in an 'old world' rhythmic prose – uniquely different.

THE STONE OF HEAVEN

THE STONE OF HEAVEN IS JADE
IN ALL ITS FORM OR COLOR
JADE'S COLD, IMPERSONAL SELF
DOES WONDER FOR THE PSYCHE

TWO DEDICATED JOURNALIST
RESEARCHED ITS ORIGIN IN THEIR BOOK;
NAMED IT – 'THE STONE OF HEAVEN'

MASSES DIED FOR A POSSESSION OF THIS STONE
EMPERORS WARRED OVER IT

UPON BIRTH, A CHINESE BABY WAS GIFTED THE MOST
PRECIOUS PIECE AVAILABLE FOR PROTECTION, PLUS A GOOD LIFE

THE DEATH OF AN EMPEROR WARRANTED AN ARMOUR OF JADE
TO PRESERVE HIS BODY
BIRTH – DEATH – BOTH RELATED TO THIS COVETED STONE

ORPHANAGE UPBRINGING WAS NOT A PLACE FOR LEARNING
ABOUT CHINA'S ANCIENT RITUALS
OR TRAPPINGS OF THE OUTER WORLD...

BUT, AT THE STORE, A NEW GIFT ITEM TOTED BY 'ALL' ARRIVED
'SIX JADE ROLLERS' FOR MASSAGING
AND IN AN INSTANT THEY WERE SOLD OUT!

FACES FELT RENEWED, A SORE NECK RELIEVED IN MINUTES
A NON-COMMITTAL, WITNESSED ALL – AND BELIEVED
A PROMISE OF GOODNESS? – THE FOUNTAIN OF YOUTH?

IT WAS – UNBELIEVABLE – PURE JOY FOR ALL
CHINA'S – 'STONE OF HEAVEN'

Facts:

The jade rollers are $14.95 each.
– High end models used this as their daily regime.
The price back then, was $100.00!
– One fellow @ the store bought it for a gift, plus one for himself!

GO WITHIN

OVERWHELMED? – A SITUATION DEEMED IMPOSSIBLE...
WHAT DOES ONE DO?
THE SPIRITUAL / METAPHYSICAL TEACHINGS EMPHASIZE;
GO WITHIN
YOU HAVE ALL THE ANSWERS! – THAT IT?
TOO EASY!
IT SIMPLY IS – LIKE A – B – C !
COME AS A CHILD – OPEN – RECEIVING – BELIEVING
OUR THOUGHTS ARE THINGS – THEY MANIFEST
CHANGE YOUR SITUATION – CHANGE YOUR LIFE!

BREATHE DEEPLY – SILENTLY PRAY / MEDITATE – QUIET THE MIND
VISUALIZE THE PERFECT OUTCOME
IT IS THE LAW OF ATTRACTION

WHERE DID THESE PRACTICES COME FROM?
NOT FROM ORPHANAGE UPBRINGING,
BORN WITH GOD'S GIFT OF AN INQUIRING MIND
TRANSFORMATION BEGAN – TRULY LISTENING TO LIFE
'MING QUONG STORE' CUSTOMERS
THEIR KNOWLEDGE
THEIR THOUGHTS – THEIR SHARED EXPERIENCES;
A FRESH PERSPECTIVE

ALSO, FROM THE ACCLAIMED – 'SECRET,' CAME:
EMPHASIS ON – 'GRATITUDE' – 'BELIEF' – AND – THE IRREPLACEABLE – 'LOVE'
DIGEST: OPRAH WINFREY'S REAFFIRMING OUTLOOK
HER IN DEPTH INTERVIEWS – WITH SPECIAL GUESTS
'PBS' – INTUITIVE PROGRAMS – INFORMED 'BOOKS'
RELIGIOUS RETREATS – 'CAMPS FARTHEST OUT'
UPLIFTING – SOOTHING MUSIC
UNITY'S, 'DAILY WORD' MAGAZINE
THE 'SCIENCE OF MIND' MAGAZINE
KNOWLEDGE COMES IN DIFFERENT SHAPES AND FORMS;
BE OPEN FOR THE UNEXPECTED – LEARN FROM EACH ENCOUNTER
REMEMBERING; TO
GO WITHIN...

SUICIDE – WHY? – 'PARTS UNKNOWN'

ANTHONY BOURDAIN COMPLETED SUICIDE – WHY?
AN OUTLANDISH CULINARY WARRIOR IN THE FOOD WORLD
'SQUEAMISH FOODS' – NOT FIT FOR HUMANS – HE BRAVELY SWALLOWED
REPULSIVENESS WAS HEARD ACROSS FOREIGN LANDS
COUNTRIES MARVELLED, THIS BRAVE SOUL WAS WITH THEM IN SPIRIT
HE CREATED INTRIGUE FOR NON-ADVENTURERS
OUR FANTASY ESCAPE — GONE

HE SURVIVED THE 60'S PITFALLS
BUT GOT LOST IN HIS WORLD
HIS CLOSE FRIENDS GONE MUCH TOO EARLY
HE PHILOSOPHISED AND WONDERED WHY...

ONCE – IN WALNUT CREEK, HE STROLLED NORTH MAIN
JUST TWO DOORS AWAY FROM MING QUONG – LOCAL PAPER CAPTURED
HIS GAZE ON THE STEPS OF THE HISTORIC WHITE HOUSE
HIS WISTFUL EYES – SEEING – BEYOND THE HORIZON
I CLIPPED THE PICTURE AND TUCKED IT AWAY
WHY? – BECAUSE HE WAS – 'ANTHONY BOURDAIN'!

HIS DEATH CAME TO ME VIA MY FRIEND – ON MY 85TH BIRTHDAY!
AS I PEPPERED, "WHY?"
WE IMMORTALIZED; THE GIFT HE GAVE

THAT NIGHT, IN A DAZE I DABBLED AT MY BIRTHDAY CHOICE –
'HONEY WALNUT PRAWNS' – IT ELUDED MY APPETITE

TONIGHT; I WAS GRATEFUL – A DISTRACTION –
THE WARRIORS / CAVALIERS BASKETBALL FINALS – WARRIORS WON
AS DID THE CULINARY WARRIOR!
SADLY, OH SO SADLY – TO – 'PARTS UNKNOWN'

Facts:

RIP Anthony 6/8/2018

CUTER THAN CUTE – BEANIE BABIES

BEANIE BABY DAYS, LIKEN TO A MARATHON
IN 50 YEARS OF RUNNING A STORE
NOTHING COMPARED, LITTLE STUFFED ANIMALS, ADORABLE, AFFORDABLE

ANNUAL SAN FRANCISCO GIFT SHOW – HAND PICKED
THE LITTLE TIE-DYE BEAR AND OTHERS...
ALL, CUTER THAN CUTE

BIG DAY – ORDER ARRIVED – THE RACE BEGAN
I RAN AND RAN, AND NEVER STOPPED RUNNING
ONE CUSTOMER RAN SO FAST, SHE FELL
RIGHT IN THE MIDDLE OF MAIN STREET

HER SPECIAL 'LAYAWAY' ORDER HAD ARRIVED – NOT STOLEN BY THE
'SUBSTITUTE' DELIVERY MAN! SUSPECTED, BUT NO PROOF!
HE WAS ALOOF – GUILTY WAS HIS NAME!

CUSTOMERS, OLD AND NEW LINED UP
THROUGH THE CONNECTED ARCHWAY TO —
JIM'S SIDE OF THE STORE AND OUT THE DOOR
PEOPLE ANXIOUS, STOOD STAUNCH, NO BUTTING IN!

BEANIE BABIES, SALES OPENED NEW DOORS IN MY LIFE
FIRST BOOK, CHOPSTICK CHILDHOOD PUBLISHED!
WON AN AWARD – FOR – 'WOMAN OF DISTINCTION'!

MET NEW CUSTOMERS, LIFELONG FRIENDS
TRADED A FEW BEANIES WITH MY NEW CHINESE FRIEND
FOR A ' BOOK READING' – AT OAKLAND'S NEW LIBRARY IN CHINATOWN
CHINATOWN FELT LIKE HOME, ALTHOUGH, THE NEW LIBRARY, SO AMERICANIZED

BEANIE BABIES SOLD EVERYWHERE – FUTURE COLLECTIBLES, NIL
THOUGH, TWO DECADES LATER, 'PRINCESS DIANA' BEAR IS A COLLECTIBLE
BACK THEN, MY MOTHER-IN-LAW RESIDED AT A REST HOME,
SHE LOVED STUFFED ANIMALS, I GAVE HER – 'PRINCESS DIANA' – SHE GLOWED
UNFORTUNATELY, THE BEAR DISAPPEARED, STOLEN?

YEARS LATER – THE ONLY BEANIE BABY I HAVE IS A TIE-DYE CAT – WHICH
I NAMED – 'JO JO' – HAND-PICKED BY A FRIEND – CUTER THAN CUTE

JO-JO – JUST LIKE A HUMAN

WHEN I CALLED JO-JO, OUR CAT – FROM THE UPPER DECK
HE CAME CHARGING BELOW, ROUNDED THE BEND
SAW ME, AND INSTANTLY HALTED, PAWS SKIDDING, EMBARRASSED
SMILING, I THOUGHT – JUST LIKE A HUMAN

ONCE, AN OVERSIZED BUDDHA FACE WAS PLACED ON THE DECK
JO-JO STARED – ENTRANCED
I ASKED, "ARE YOU MEDITATING?"
HE IGNORED ME, CONCENTRATING ON BUDDHA'S FACE
HE WAS MEDITATING – JUST LIKE A HUMAN !

A TREAT FOR JO-JO – THEN OFF TO WORK
A SOFT CONNECTION, AS HE WHISPERED, "MEOW"
LEANING INTO HIS BLACK AND WHITE FUR
HIS BREATH ABATED, AS I SPOKE,
"I HAVE TO GO TO WORK NOW…"
SO SWEET, SO SOFT, SO LOVING
THE SOUL OF A CAT

SOME TIME LATER, – TREAT TIME
NO RESPONSE – WAITED – STILL NO RESPONSE
CONCERNED, BUT NOT TOO WORRIED

THEN, I GLIMPSED JO-JO UNDER THE DECK
STRETCHED OUT IN RUNNING FORM
LIFELESS AND RIGID – WHEN HAD HE DIED?
IT SEEMED HE TRIED TO SAY HIS LAST – 'GOOD-BYE'

PRECIOUS JO JO
THE SOUL OF A CAT FELT
FOREVER IN OUR HEARTS

I FOUND A SOFT SPOT, RICH IN NUTRIENTS FOR HIM
WITH A 'PLANT-OF-LIFE' ATOP HIS PLOT
IN HIS QUIET ZEN LIKE WAY, HIS PRESENCE IS FELT
JUST LIKE A HUMAN…

YAY — WARRIORS

WARRIORS – WHO ARE THEY?
FROM DAYS OF OLD? FIGHTING MEN?
OH – YOU MEAN — THE NBA – NATIONAL BISCUIT ASSOCIATION?
NO! – 'DUBS, DUBS' — DOES THAT MEAN – 'DUMB, DUMB'?
NO – IT MEANS – 'THE OAKLAND BASKETBALL PLAYERS,' THEM NBA PEOPLE!

OH THEM OAKLAND GUYS! WHO ARE NOT SHY – MOVING AWAY – ACROSS THE
BAY
YET — AM TRULY WITH THEM ALL THE WAY
BECAUSE OF – 'STEPH CURRY' – WHO SEEMS NOT TO BE IN A HURRY
BUT – DOES SCURRY HERE AND THERE
IN FACT – USUALLY – LATE — THE LAST ONE IN!
BETTER IN – THAN OUT! - HE'S 100% 'REAL'… HE'S THE REAL DEAL…
THIS PROSEY POEM IS SLIGHTLY WACKY, OR MAYBE TACKY
AND EVEN KIND OF RHYMES? – THIS EVOLVED. BECAUSE OF A WAKER-UPPER
A DOCTOR'S VISIT! - REALIZED LIFE'S TOO SHORT
THEREFORE – A NONSENSE POEM – OR IS IT 'NO-NONSENSE'?!
I MAY FLUNK OR GO KERPLUNK – BUT WON'T BE IN A FUNK!
BESIDES, THIS COULD BE FUN – LIKE A DAY IN THE SUN!

I PLAYED BASKETBALL ONCE, 'THE GIRL'S WAY' WHILE AT OAKLAND HIGH
RECALLED, A GIRL'S DISTORTED FACE – HER FIERCENESS STARTLED ME
GEEZ, I THOUGHT, – "WHY SO MEAN-LOOKING!?"
I WAS JUST CATCHING THE BALL THAT'S ALL – ISN'T THAT THE OBJECT, THE
BALL?
YES, I KNOW – SCORING A BASKET IS – TOP PRIORITY!
TO THIS DAY, I STILL SEE HER EXPRESSION! - IT'S HAUNTING!
LIKE THEM WARRIORS – THEIR FACES – DAUNTING!

LOVE THEM WARRIORS! – BASKETBALL KNOWLEDGE LOOMING
'FLUBS' OR WAS THAT 'DUBS?' – THE 'SPLASH' BROTHERS – NOT 'FLASHERS'
BUT SNEAK-PEAK THEM MUSCLES BENEATH THEM TANKS! – WOW HUH?

NICKNAMED A FEW PLAYERS, JUST FOR FUN – BUT – ONE COULD BE A PUN!
'HOW'S 'SLEEPY HEAD?' – FOR DEAR OLE BOGUT – DOES HE NOT LOOK SLEEPY?
AT LEAST – HE'S NOT CREEPY
THEN – THERE'S JEREBKO – 'WHITENESS' – THE ONLY WHITE GUY ON THE
TEAM!
WHY? – BECAUSE HE'S LEAN AND MEAN? – NO – DUMB DUMB!
HE'S GOT IT – OR HE'S WOULDN'T BE ON THE TEAM – I KNOW — I TRULY DO
SOMETIMES MY EYES DECEIVE ME
LIKE – WHO JUST SCORED?
WAS THAT KLAY OR WAS THAT CURRY?
MISTOOK THEM BOTH FOR 'WHITENESS'!
BLACK OR WHAT, THEY'RE ALL THE SAME — THEY'RE OUR SAVIOUR,

I MEAN WARRIORS — GEEZ, IT DOESN'T REALLY RHYME!
THOUGH THE 'WORD'
ALMOST LOOK ALIKE! –
BUT – WHO SAYS IT HAS TO FIT
THEY'LL SAVE OUR SKIN – NO MATTER WHAT
MAKES NO DIFFERENCE – THEY PLAY TO WIN
WITH NO FLAGRANT SIN!
WHEN THE 'OTHER' TEAM HAS THE BALL – CROWD SHOUTS, – 'DEFENSE'
I SHOUT – 'MISS!' – WHY? BECAUSE THEY HAVE THE BALL!   DUH!!!
ONE CAN HEAR ME SHOUT — 'IN' — WHEN THEM WARRIORS HAVE THE BALL
YES — I'M WAY AHEAD OF THE PLAY LIKE A SMART-ALECK STUDENT
'GO TO THE HEAD OF THE CLASS!' OR – YOU – THERE! – 'SIT THEE DOWN!'
OFTEN I SHOUT – "FINALLY!" WHEN A POINT IS FINALLY MADE
NOT BEGGING – JUST EGGING THEM ON!
SO — GO – WARRIORS GO – SET A NEW RECORD WITHOUT COUSINS!
COUSIN? WHO'S HE? — RELATED TO WHOM?
OH, THE NEW WARRIOR WHO'S BEEN ON HIS BUN TOO LONG!
POOR GUY – HIS SKILLS NEVER UTILIZED – AT LEAST HE WASN'T EULOGIZED!
REMORSE FOLLOWED HIS DEMISE – THOUGH I SURMISED HIS RHYTHM FINE
AS WE WATCHED HIM WHILE WE DINED
I DID SO WANT TO SEE HIS VICTORIOUS FACE WHEN THEM WARRIORS RAISED
THEIR FIST UPWARDS – SUGGESTING – 'JUSTICE FOR ALL' – HUH?
OH MY GOSH — WRONG ERA! — WRONG GAME! — WRONG EVERYTHING!
NO MATTER — LET'S ALL 'RANT FOR: DURANT' — LET'S SHOUT FOR:
GREEN – IGUODALA – LIVINGSTON – LOONEY – LEE – COOK, AND McKINNIE
PLUS, OF COURSE – COACH KERR AS THEY RAISE THEIR FIST VICTORIOUSLY
WHILE WE CHEER GLORIOUSLY
"YAY WARRIORS — OUR SAVIOUR!"

Facts:

In (2019) this 'prosey' poem composed during the 'playoffs,' took 2 pages – a 1st! My goal, 'one' page, as this method was new to me. Whatever the 'outcome' for the semi-finals, I couldn't include, as I was on my formatter's schedule. Which brings to mind, when the Currys lived in Walnut Creek, our mail carrier had delivered mail to his home, & had dialogue with Curry and Bogut – In anticipation, I happily had a 'Welcome to Walnut Creek' gift for the Curry family; my 1st book, *Chopstick Childhood*, to be delivered to a family member – but that never came to fruition! Maybe someday – he'll venture in…

– Remember when Curry made a TV commercial atop the hills of San Francisco's Chinatown at the 'Cameron House' basketball courts? Excitement for the young ones – who disobeyed orders, they talked to him!

Note: poem written when Jerebko –'Whiteness'– was 'the one & only'!

A MOTHER'S PRIDE

'GRACEFUL – AND — OH – SO BEAUTIFUL
DELICATE AND FRAGILE
HER BEING – SHY AND QUIET – AS THE NIGHT'

WORDS FROM THE CARD ARTIST – JANE STONE
DESCRIBED MY MOTHER – SHE CONTINUED:
'A SADNESS ENVELOPED HER.'

JANE HAD ENCOUNTERED HER ONCE BEFORE
WHEN SHE DESIGNED – THE 'NONA NECKLACE' – LATE AT NIGHT
JANE HAD TRIED TO COMMUNICATE – NO WORDS CAME FORTH
MOTHER CONVEYED FEELINGS WITH HEARTFELT EXPRESSIONS

ANOTHER CHINESE WOMAN – A PSYCHIC SPOKE TO HER;
THE MESSAGE – "I AM SORRY, I AM VERY PROUD OF HER!"
I HEARD – I LISTENED – AND SAID — "NOTHING!" WHY? PUZZLED, WAS I
IT SEEMED – MARLENE'S DIALECT WAS HER TONGUE
FOR JANE, AN ORPHAN – WOULD IT HAVE BEEN DIFFERENT?

'ACCEPTANCE' FROM ME, FOR HER ABANDONMENT OF YESTERYEARS
HAD VANISHED FROM MY MIND, MANY MOONS AGO
AS IN MY BOOKS, NOW, HER COMMENT SILENCED ME!
WHY WAS SHE PROUD OF ME?
I ONLY DID WHAT I COULD DO; — AT 2 YEARS OF AGE — I SURVIVED!

IS AN 'OLD-WORLD' CHINESE WOMAN TRULY PROUD?
AS IN THE ANCIENT CULTURE — FEELINGS KEPT UNDER WRAP
BUT – SHE WAS NOT THE NORM — FEISTY WAS SHE, WITH HER IN-LAWS

ARE 'OLD THOUGHTS' DIMINISHED IN THE AFTERLIFE?
THEN — EVER SO SILENTLY — THE LIGHT DAWNED
THIS POEM — REVEALED TRANSPARENCY!
IT REVEALED HER PROUDNESS
MY MOTHER HAD INSTILLED IN ME
WHAT WAS IMBUED IN HER — 'RESILIENCEY'

Facts:

The 1st psychic, Jane Stone, was an award-winning card maker. She created, the 'Nona' necklace – to honor my 1st book, – *Chopstick Childhood*. Her story and the necklace is pictured in the *Ten Thousand Flowers* book. – Marlene Hoy, known for her psychic abilities, had a private practice. She was the wife of Walter Hoy, former principal of Miramonte High School, both respected individuals in the community.

BABY CLOUD AT PLAY

EARLY MORNING – MT. DIABLO'S VIEW – DISTRACTED
A BABY CLOUD, PRISTINE WHITE, SLIDING DOWN
THE – 'FRONT' – OF THE MOUNTAIN

MAMA CLOUD WHISPERED;
"WHAT ARE YOU DOING?,
YOU ARE DISTRACTING THE VIEW!"

"HOW MAMA?"
ALL OF US CLOUDS HAVE TO BE – 'BEHIND' – THE MOUNTAIN
WE TAKE CARE OF THE BACKGROUND
OUR DUTY – TO KEEP MT. DIABLO'S VIEW – PICTURE-PERFECT

FLOAT YOURSELF UP TO THE TOP
AND SLIDE OVER THE BACK
BABY CLOUD LIFTED HER LITTLE SELF UP

IN DOING SO – BABY CLOUD SEEMED TO GET
THINNER AND THINNER
DISAPPEARING INTO A LIGHT HAZE

BABY CLOUD BEGAN TO CRY
"MAMA, MAMA – HELP ME
I'M GETTING WEAKER…"

MAMA'S HEART PITIED THE TINY CLOUD
TENDERLY – WITH A PROMISE – FROM BABY CLOUD
TO REMEMBER OUR DUTY!

MAMA CLOUD SUMMONED TWO GOOD FRIENDS TO HELP…
THE 'WIND' – BLEW THE VAST CLOUDS
ACROSS MT. DIABLO — TILL
MISTY FOG COVERED THE MOUNTAIN TOP
BABY CLOUD FLOATED UP – BEHIND THE MOUNTAIN
MAMA CLOUD AND BABY CLOUD SMILED
THEIR FRIEND, THE 'SUN,' – SPREAD IT'S WARM RAYS
DISSOLVING THE FOGGY COVER
ONCE AGAIN – MT. DIABLO – PICTURE PERFECT

Reflection:

– Fortunate, am I, to have a view of Mt. Diablo.

CHINA WALL – ON MT. DIABLO

NEWS TO ME! — A CHINA WALL?
WAY – WAY – WAY – UP THERE IN THE SKY
WHO ARE WE PROTECTING? OR — WHO IS OUR ENEMY?
UNLIKE A 'TRUMP' WALL
DEMANDED – BY THE UNITED STATES PRESIDENT

NATURAL – GEOLOGIC BOULDERS
CRAGGY – SANDSTONE ROCKS
RESEMBLED A MINIATURE WALL

STRONG – AS FORMED BY ROCK OF AGES
NO ENEMIES, SKYHIGH
WE ARE SAFE! — FREE FROM INVISIBLE INVADERS

BIKE UP TO MT. DIABLO
FANTASTIC — ONE CAN ALMOST SEE FARAWAY CHINA
AND THEIR GREAT WALL!
MARVEL AT OUR CHINA WALL

ONE BIKER – FILMED ON VIDEO
OUT OF BREATH – CAUGHT HIS SECOND WIND
MISCHIEVOUSLY CREDITED

OUR CHINA WALL
TO A CHINESE WOMAN ON-LOOKER
ADORNED IN A UNIQUE ASIAN TOP

EVER SO HUMBLE
SHE SHRANK INTO HER SHELL
A TOUCH OF THE 'OLD-WORLD' TRANSPOSED

YET – HEARD TO MURMUR;
"ALL MADE BY HAND –
A GIFT FROM CHINA!"

NEWS, TO ME!
— "THANK YOU, CHINA ..."

Facts:

Mt. Diablo with China Wall on the 2019, Watershed calendar.
Stephen Joseph, photo. "Thanks" to Brian Murphy for his knowledge.
Geologist from around the world visit this site.
'China Wall' is used for special events...

1ˢᵀ WOMAN ARCHITECT

JULIA MORGAN
CALIFORNIA'S – 1ˢᵀ – DESIGNED THE
1ˢᵀ OFFICIAL - 'MING QUONG HOME'
THEY KNEW – THIS WOMAN HAD
THE FAITH – THE LOVE – THE COMMITMENT

CULTURE FOR THE YOUNG ONES
INSTILLED TOUCHES OF ANCIENT CHINA
COURTYARD — GOLD FISHES IN THE POND
FLOATING PINK LOTUS — SYMBOLIC IMAGES
IN FRONT — COMMANDING STAIRS
LEAD TO A SPACIOUS GLASS/FRAMED LIVING ROOM, TRIMMED
WITH BERNARD MAYBECK'S SIGNATURE – DARK, EARTHY WOOD
THIS MANSION FIT FOR THE EMPEROR OF CHINA
WAS FAR REMOVED FROM HER MIND
THIS 'LOVE-AFFAIR' WAS FOR THE NEEDY — CHINESE – ORPHAN – GIRLS

JULIA'S GIFT;
TWO ROYAL-BLUE 'FU-DOGS' STATUES – ATOP THE STAIRS
PROTECTED THE CHILDREN – DAY AND NIGHT
THE CHILDREN ADORED THESE GIANT TRADITIONAL DOGS
GLEEFULLY RIDING THEM AT PLAY
TO LIVE LIKE ROYALTY, AMONGST THEIR NEW ABODE
SURROUNDED BY EUCALYPTUS TREES – AND A MEANDERING CREEK
ONE WOULD NEVER BELIEVE, ORPHANS LIVED THERE
THESE CHERISHED MEMORIES – ARE FOREVER REMEMBERED
GRATEFUL FOR THEIR 'CULTURAL – INHERITANCE'

YEARS LATER – 'MING QUONG' ALUMNI ENJOYED THIS SITE
FOR MEMORABLE REUNIONS...
JULIA MORGAN – 1ˢᵀ, IN SPIRIT – STRONG IN WILL – A FRIEND INDEED

Facts / Reflections:

Privileged to have had my 1ˢᵗ book, *Chopstick Childhood* reading at this historic site. The MQH adjacent to Mills College in Oakland, CA, was once acquired by Mills for expansion. Today known as the 'Julia Morgan Middle School,' a school for girls. – Numerous sites designed by Morgan (who studied under Bernard Maybeck): SF-Chinatown YWCA; the Asilomar Conference Ctr. in Monterey; plus Hearst Castle in San Simeon. – Many awards – 1ˢᵗ, in 1904 – for 1ˢᵗ woman architect, in CA – Lastly – posthumously awarded – American Institute of Architects of Gold Medal, a 1ˢᵗ for a woman, in 2014.

Note: The former MQH site — donated by Stanley Dollar, of the Dollar Steamship Line. The story is in the *Bamboo Women* book.

CHINESE RAILROAD
AT THE ROSE BOWL PARADE

150 SUCCESSFUL YEARS PASSED – HISTORY DOCUMENTED
CHINESE IMMIGRANTS HONORED
FOR RAILROAD CONTRIBUTION
CALIFORNIA'S CELEBRATED EVENT ON A ROYAL DAY
NEW YEAR'S DAY – THE ACCLAIMED – ROSE BOWL PARADE
WHERE FRAGRANT ROSES BLUSHED WITH LOVE

THE BRAND NEW YEAR – '2019' – IN PASADENA, CALIFORNIA
THE SOUTHERN CALIFORNIA SUN
REFLECTED – 'GOLD MOUNTAIN'
BEAMED RAYS OF HEALING WARMTH
TOWARDS GENERATIONS OF REMEMBRANCES
THOUSANDS OF VIEWERS FROM AROUND THE WORLD
THE COLORFUL CHINESE FLOAT — 'HARMONY THROUGH UNION'
REPLICA – OF THE – TRANSCONTINENTAL RAILWAY
ARTWORK REPRESENTED CHINA'S CULTURE
PRANCING LIONS MARKED THE DAY'S JOY – FACES GLOWED

SUDDENLY – FIRE! – WHITE SMOKE BILLOWED
UNDER THE ENORMOUS STRUCTURE
EMERGENCY CREW SCURRIED AND SWARMED
LIKE HONEY BEES PROTECTING THEIR QUEEN BEE

UNPREDICTABLE, YIN AND YANG
ALL ABOARD THE FLOAT – EVERYONE SAFE – PARADE STOPPED TEMPORARILY
"TOP OF THE NEWS," — EXTENSIVE COVERAGE
WILL THE CHINESE EVER, TRULY SHARE
THEIR CONTRIBUTION TO AMERICA?

OMINOUSLY – FATE DEALT A WINNING HAND!
AS WHO COULD RECALL, THE PRIZE-WINNING FLOAT OF 2019?
PAR TO NONE – MOST VIEWERS – RECALL, THE DRAMA
THE RAILROAD FLOAT ON FIRE – RESCUE CREWS DOUSING THE FLOAT
MEMORIES REMEMBERED – A GLORIOUS CITY, VACATION WEATHER,
LINGERING PERFUMED ROSES – THE LAST RAYS OF THE SINKING SUN
FLOAT PERFORMERS EVER GRATEFUL
THEIR CONTRIBUTION – SEARED MEMORABLY!

Facts:

Rose Bowl Parade – 1/2/2019. The Chinese immigrants toiled and blasted through solid rocks and rugged terrain. Picks, shovels, horses and wheelbarrows–their tools. 15,000 laborers etched out close to 2,000 miles for the Transcontinental Railroad. Thousands died for the 'Taming of the Wild West.' Businesses boomed, California now historically connected to the East Coast.

BELIEVE — ACHIEVE

'TWO' ALUMNI OF THE MING QUONG HOME ACHIEVED THEIR GOAL
WITH THEIR BAMBOO SPIRIT
THEY PERSEVERED, DELETED THE INFAMOUS WORD;
'PROSTITUTES'
FROM THE INNOCENCE OF YOUTH

MING QUONG'S NAME REPUTEDLY INTACT
THE SANITY OF MQ ALUMNI – AND –
THE MING QUONG STORE IN WALNUT CREEK
ARE RADIANT
AS IT SHOULD BE;
FOR 'MING QUONG,' IN CANTONESE MEANS
'RADIANT LIGHT'

BEHIND THESE TWO WOMEN WERE DEDICATED
MING QUONG ALUMNI
THEIR ENCOURAGEMENT AND BELIEF COMPELLED THEM ON
EARNEST CONVERSATIONS;
WITH UPLIFT FAMILY SERVICES
BOTH PARTIES AGREED

THE ORIGINATORS AND TEACHERS OF THE MING QUONG HOME
CAN NOW REST IN PEACE
AS EACH STEP CORRECTED – FOSTERS AMERICA'S TRUE HISTORY
AMEN – AMEN...

Facts: 11/17/2018 –

Elena Wong, Janet Chang of the MQH – along with Lisa Alegria, of Uplift Family Services – corrected & wrote a special amendment for the complete history of Ming Quong in Los Gatos & Oakland for Uplift's records. This will be distributed to the Los Gatos 'NuMu' Museum, Colleges with Asian Studies courses, & the Press. Uplift Family Services websites will also be corrected. – Facts / stories of the above 'discrepancies' are in the *Bamboo Women* book.

Special thanks to Greg, former D.A. (son of former MQ alumnae), for his help in editing and adding credence to rewrite MQ history.

WORDS HAVE SPOKEN

PRECIOUS GEMS ARE THEY – THE SPOKEN WORDS
FROM THE 1ST BABBLINGS OF AN INFANT
THE BEGINNING OF LIFE

MOTHERS MAY WHISPER ENDEARMENTS
PLANT A LOVING HUG; BUT NO WORDS SPOKEN
YET – BABIES FEEL THE LOVE …
AS LOVE EXPANDS – TO WORDS – TO BOOKS …TO UNDERSTANDING
LITTLE MINDS MESMERISED

STORIES AS ONLY WORDS CAN PORTRAY
PLACED CAREFULLY IN SENTENCES
EACH CHOICE WORD, SETS OUR MIND TO SOAR
TO MEANDER TO LIFE BEYOND
LIKE A BIRD IN FLIGHT – ALL OUR SENSES OPEN TO THE WIND

THOUGHTS FROM WORDS
PROFOUND – SAD – OR – HUMOROUS
ARE IN ONE'S THOUGHTS
AS WORDS HAVE SPOKEN

READ A POEM OR A BOOK
TO THE INFIRMED – TO THE SIGHTLESS
YOU ARE THEIR EYES
GRATEFUL TEARS MAY FLOW – FEEL THEIR LOVE

SOME MAY LISTEN QUIETLY, RESTING – ENERGY WANED
YET – GRASPING EACH SPOKEN WORD
YOUR DEDICATION COMES THROUGH
THEY FEEL YOUR LOVE
AS WORDS HAVE SPOKEN

Reflections:

Friend, Maure Quilter, initials 'MQ' author,
and an avid reader, is now sightless!

Audios & 'people/readers' are now a joyful part
of her life. She feels blessed…

Her favorite motto: "We're all just walking
each other home." – Ram Dass

THERE ARE NO 'FREE' LUNCHES

BUT – I – WAS INVITED TO A 'FREE' LUNCH!
BY THE KIWANIS CLUB OF WALNUT CREEK
TO CELEBRATE MY ARTICLE – 'MEMORIES OF WALNUT CREEK'
WRITTEN BY THE – WALNUT CREEK HISTORICAL SOCIETY
SO THERE I WAS — GREETED BY PETE, THE SECRETARY
HAPPY TO ONCE AGAIN BE WITH THE FRIENDLIEST PEOPLE
ON THE 'BOOK-READING' CIRCUIT – HUGS – GENUINE SMILES SIGNIFIED,
I HAD ARRIVED – AND THE COMMENT: "YOU'RE OUR – SPECIAL GUEST
WE CAN'T WAIT TO HEAR YOU TALK!"
HUH?!? – OH MY GOSH — UNPREPARED WAS I
ABSOLUTELY NOTHING PLANNED!
SECRETARY ASKED, "WHAT IS YOUR CHOICE FOR LUNCH? IT'S FREE."
DAVE – BLURTED, "THERE ARE NO FREE LUNCHES!"
INSTANT TRANSPARENCY! – NOW, FOR THE MENU – BUT
AN ITALIAN WORD STUMPED ME – REPLIED, "CAN'T MAKE UP MY MIND,
I'LL TAKE BOTH!" – SILENCE! – SHE'S OUR GUEST! – IS SHE FOR REAL?
'SPAG…' THE LIGHT DAWNED! – MY PICK. – 'SPAGHETTI BOLOGNESE'
DELICIOUS – TRUE ITALIAN! – WAY, BEYOND MY HOME COOKING!
AFTER LUNCH – ALL EYES ON ME!
ONE QUESTION ASKED – "TELL US ABOUT YOUR 'ROYALTY'"
THE STORY UNFOLDED GENUINELY – NATURALLY
ONCE AGAIN – AMAZED, WAS I – BY THE
DISCOVERY OF – 'MY ANCIENT ROYALTY' – PLUS NOW – ANOTHER
WONDERMENT!

REALIZATION – THIS 'FREE LUNCH' – SET ME FREE! – 'TO BE IN THE MOMENT'
TO BE 'MYSELF' – TO UNFOLD – TO BANTER FREELY
PLUS, LATER ABLE TO RECALL – THOUGHTS FOR THIS 'PROSEY' POEM!
PERHAPS, 'THERE ARE NO FREE LUNCHES' BUT – WHAT WAS LEARNED; WAS
'PRICELESS!' – I WAS SET 'FREE', TO MAKE 'A JOYFUL NOISE UNTO THE LORD!'
OH MY GOSH – 'FROM THE DEPTH OF MY SOUL, AN UNEXPECTED 'BIBLICAL'
VERSE!'
THE LORD WORKS IN MYSTERIOUS WAYS! DID THIS POEM OPEN A NEW DOOR?
OR REVEREND BOB'S PRESENCE EVOKED NEW AVENUES? ONLY TIME WILL TELL
MY 'DEEPEST' APPRECIATION – FOR THE – WALNUT CREEK KIWANIS CLUB...

Reflections:

Lunch @ Massimo's Restaurant, with Pete Schmitt, Secretary (I was his guest)
Jim Cole, President – Dave Kwinter, former recruiter for guest speakers,
Reverend Bob Williams, retired Presbyterian minister, acquainted with the
Ming Quong Home. Treasurer, Greg Hunter, Paul Miller, asst., Dr. Ron Grafton,
Wil Roberge. Women members, unfortunately, under the weather. My knee not
up to par, Dave escorted me to the 'free lunch!' 'Witty,' every second, laughter
was my 'joy!'

"WHO IS - SALVATOR MUNDI?"

I KNEW A SALVADOR SANCHEZ, IN GRADE SCHOOL
SPELLED WITH A 'D' - NOW - THIS NAME INTRIGUED ME!
SALVATOR MUNDI? AFTER I READ THE PAPERS I REALIZED
I KNEW HIM! — I HAD BEEN RAISED WITH HIM AS A CHILD!
HE HAD BEEN BESIDE ME ALL THE TIME - ALL THE WAY!
I KNEW HIM AS 'JESUS'
JESUS OF NAZARETH
SON OF MARY AND JOSEPH

LEONARDO DA VINCI, THE WORLD-FAMOUS PAINTER
KNEW HIM AS 'SALVATOR MUNDI' - HIS PAINTING OF
SALVATOR MUNDI SOLD FOR $450. 3 MILLION
THE MOST EXPENSIVE WORK AT AN AUCTION

CONNECTED — WERE WE!
MY PORTRAIT OF MY - 'NEW JESUS,' SKETCHED WITH BLACK CHARCOAL
SOLD FOR $25.00 AT THE BIBLE BOOK STORE
'COPIES' SOLD AS - 'LOVE OFFERINGS' - WHAT YOUR 'HEART' FELT
HIGHEST LOVE OFFERING - $15.00
WHAT DID THESE ARTISTS HAVE IN COMMON?
BOTH, RARITY WORKS OF ART - IN THEIR OWN RIGHTS

THEIR IMAGE IMPACTED THEIR BUYER;
FOR - CROWN PRINCE, MOHAMMED BIN SALMAN - PRESTIGIOUSNESS
YOUTH RELATED TO 'NEW JESUS - LIVES WERE TURNED AROUND
THESE PORTRAITS NOT ON DISPLAY — WHY?
SALVATOR MUNDI MISSING IN 2017 - LOUVRE SHOW
- CANCELLED - NO EXPLANATION
A MYSTERY - THE ART WORLD TURNED UPSIDE DOWN!
THE 'NEW JESUS' — SOLD OUT SUMMERS AGO, DURING AN 'EXPRESSIVE' ERA
ARE THERE LESSONS ABOUT THESE COMPARISONS? - PERHAPS - AS IN;
THE PARADOXES OF LIFE ... EACH SITUATION - UNIQUELY DIFFERENT
TOUCHED BY HIS LOVE, AS IN - 'TOUCHED BY THE HEM OF HIS GARMENT'
THEIR 'FAITH' - HIS FAITH - TRANSFERRED TO THEE...
'SALVATOR MUNDI' — THE 'NEW JESUS'

Facts / Reflections:

The New York Times story: "Few works of art have evoked such intrigue among the Persian Gulf royals. Louvre in Paris, eager to include Salvator Mundi in 2019 to coincide with da Vinci's 500th anniversary of his death…" Nona's Jesus drawing – over 50 years since its conception, offered a new approach to the Camp Farthest Out retreat & the cover of their summer brochure in Boulder Creek, CA in 1968. – The Jesus portrait is in the *Ten Thousand Flowers* book.

TALENTED EDITOR

(omg) – OH MY GOSH, – AUTHOR OF THREE BOOKS, AM I
ERRORS IN ABUNDANCE ON TWO NEWSLETTERS
ABBREVIATED WORDS – PERFECT
MING QUONG CUSTOMERS ARE WITH ME!
I SURMISE! YET – ONE SPOKE OUT, LOUD AND CLEAR

SUBJECT LINE;
AN UNPARDONABLE SIN
MISSPELLED WORD
THAT DID IT
ALL OUT – LESSONS
"TAKE YOUR TIME"
"TOO HARD TO READ"
"BE COGNIZANT OF YOUR READERS!"

WHO WAS THIS CRITIC?
A FRIEND
A FORMER CUSTOMER
AN EDITOR, REPORTER, AUTHOR
'PERSONALITY PLUS' FOR DECADES

I LISTENED – SLOWED DOWN
'HASTE MAKES WASTE'
NOW!! – IS MY STYLE STILL RECOGNIZABLE?
THE SAME 'OLE ME — SHORTCUTS — 'NO!'
UNLESS MY FINGERS FORGET
LET ALONE MY MIND!

THE 'TALENTED EDITOR?' – WHO CHASTISED
SUCH UNREADABLE PROSE
NONE OTHER THAN:
– 'BEN FONG TORRES' –
HELPFUL, – 'YES' – THAT'S WHAT FRIENDS ARE FOR!

Reflections:

Newsletters 1 & 2 for 2019: Chinese New Year's –
'Golden Pig with Valentines Day.'

Grateful for Ben, for slowing me down! Years ago, he endorsed my 1st book, *Chopstick Childhood* & my 2nd book, *Bamboo Women* with just one word, – 'Compelling!' –

"Thank you, Ben..."

EVENING WITH THE MASTER

AN EVENING WITH THE MASTER — JERRY BALL
THE MASTER OF ALL POEMS - SHORT OR LONG
TRADITIONAL AND HAIKU
WINNER IN AMERICA AND JAPAN
FORMER PRESIDENT OF THE HAIKU SOCIETY
CURATOR FOR THE ARCHIVES IN SACRAMENTO
ENOUGH TITLES HERE IN AMERICA - FOR THE 'HALL OF FAME!'

A SHARING HEART - HE DONATES HIS TIME - PRIVILEGED - TO BE AT HIS HOME
JUST HIM, AND I SHARING - BANTERING - MOSTLY I, ABSORBING
WHY JUST ME? - ALL OTHER POETS - OBLIGATIONS!
TONIGHT - HE READ LONG POEMS TO COINCIDE WITH MY POEMS
IN ACTUALITY, THIS TIME AND PLACE WAS MY 1ST - TRUE - LESSON IN POETRY!
FROM HIS 'LESSON PLANS' - RULES GALORE!
ADJUSTING MY MIND TO WHAT MY HEART FELT - PROMISED HOPE!

HIS HAIKU DELIGHTED ME; MY SOUL RESPONDED - WITH JOYOUS LAUGHTER

THE MASTER'S HAIKU:
A SPIRAL / THE SPIDER CONTINUES / HER MEMOIRS

AS IN THE SPIRAL - SOME WEBS - EXQUISITE - LIKE FINE LACE
OTHERS - DISTRACTING - STICK LIKE GLUE — ANNOYING!
WE CONTINUED; WITH MY POEMS AND EVEN 'ONE PROSEY ESSAY!'
AN ESSAY? - HE EXPLAINED! - AM LEARNING MORE EACH DAY!
AT A MERE - 85!
TUTORED BY JERRY - MILLENIUM YEARS AHEAD OF ME
LIKE THE WISE OLD OWL - HE IS
NOW - A QUESTION:
"AM I - OLD ENOUGH TO KNOW BETTER - YOUNG ENOUGH NOT TO CARE?"
"ABSOLUTELY - YES!"
WITH THE MASTER'S GUIDANCE - "I'M ALMOST HOME!" - THAT IS;
TRADITIONAL POEMS WITH SOME 'PROSEYS' - THEN, I'M HOME!
YAY - FOR HOME IS WHERE THE HEART IS ...

Reflections:

Some poems are kept in the present tense — in order to be
'in the present moment.'
– Memorable evening, with Jerry, his wife, Sandy & their
two chihuahua dogs. From their garden, a sprig of 'daphne,'
my favorite fragrance! Plus a large colored photo of
'Daphnes' from Jerry's collection, a photographer was he!
Also, his 'instruction pamphlet for poems!' Truly, a

Photo by
LaDonna Fehlberg

memorable 'Ball'... Facts about Jerry in all my books. NOTE: Sandy turned off
the background music – was able to comprehend Jerry's lesson, despite his
Parkinson, ever grateful.

ROYALTY NOW

INHERITED — ROYALTY
ROYALTY AS IN;
'PROSEY' POEMS

REVEALING LIFE
IN DEPTH
STRONG — STEADFAST

ROYALTY — LIKEN TO VELVET
SOOTHING THE SENSES
LUXURIOUS AS LIFE CAN BE

CHINA'S ROYALTY
MINDFULNESS OF THE AGES
LEGACY FOLLOWED...

ROYALTY IN EVERYDAY LIFE
TOGETHER WE MERGE
ROYALTY NOW...

Reflections:

'Proseys' for *Born on the 8th* were inspired partly by the Emperor's 'Gratitude'.

2,000 years later, my Life's journey took me on this poetic path, as I followed my ancestor's footsteps, Mock Chai, who published a book of poems.
His story is in my 3rd book: *Ten Thousand Flowers*.

MING QUONG'S 1ST –
ROSIE THE RIVETER

IN MY MIND – BETTY REID – WAS THE 1ST ROSIE THE RIVETER
AN ORIGINAL
MING QUONG CUSTOMER

BUT AS BETTY SAID, "THAT WAS NOT ME,
THAT'S A WHITE WOMEN'S STORY"…

BETTY SPOKE WITH HONESTY

SOON – BETTY REID BECAME
THE 'INSPIRATION' FOR 'ROSIE THE RIVETER'
POWERFUL WAS SHE

A WOMAN OF COLOR
AN UNFORGETTABLE 'BLACK BEAUTY'
LIKEN TO A MODEL FOR STRIKING LOOKS

BETTY WAS INDEED DARING
1ST BLACK WOMAN WITH HER YOUNG SON
TO ENTER THE MING QUONG STORE
A BRAVE VENTURE BACK THEN

SHE SPOKE FOR SOCIAL JUSTICE TO SOLD-OUT CROWDS
RECEIVED – ACCOLADES – AWARDS – PLUS – A SPECIAL COIN
FROM PRESIDENT BARACK OBAMA

BETTY REID'S – RADIANT LIGHT CONTINUES

— 9/23/2019

Facts:

98 years of age – the Betty Reid Soskin poem
was inspired by the passing of the original 'white'
riveter, in 2018. I vividly remember Betty Reid
and her adorable son, 'way back when,' as they
touched my heart. These unforgettable moments
are captured in my 1st book, *Chopstick Childhood*.

50 YEARS LATER — BIGGEST SURPRISE EVER

MING QUONG — THE NAME OF THE STORE
NAMED AFTER THE CHINESE GIRL'S ORPHANAGE
WHERE I WAS RAISED

THE STORE MEANS — RADIANT LIGHT
SPIRITUALITY
ACADEMICALLY — IT MEANS, BRILLIANT, BRIGHT, SHINY

WHEN A NEW CUSTOMER COMES IN
I OFTEN ASK, "DO YOU KNOW WHAT MING QUONG MEANS?"
ANSWER, "NO." — SO, I PROCEED…

THIS TIME, TO A BLOND WOMAN
SHE STOPPED ME AFTER I SAID, "RADIANT LIGHT"
AND WHAT SHE SAID, I COULDN'T BELIEVE

CAUSED MY EYES TO WIDEN
CAUSED MY EARS TO STRAIN HARDER — AND
CAUSED ME TO ASK FOR A REPEAT

BLOND WOMAN REPEATED IT MORE THAN TWICE
MY SURPRISED MIND — FINALLY UNDERSTOOD
AS I MARVELED;

SHE STATED, "THAT'S WHAT MY NAME – MEANS
— RADIANT LIGHT —

MY NAME IS – 'NIA'
YES — IT'S GAELIC — AN IRISH NAME!"

Facts:

Taylor (part-time employee) heard it all — her comment — "Cool!"
She helped me get over my OMG surprise! — I did some research on "Nia," and
Gaelic and my conclusion — Ming Quong's — "Radiant Light' came from
Donaldina Cameron, herself! Who else, but she, could use such beautiful,
expressive words? My MQ customers have always been enamored by the
meaning. They feel 'it' and leave content.

ALMOST ON FIRE!

FIFTY YEARS AGO – IN AN OLD WALNUT CREEK HOTEL LOBBY
I RAN A SMALL STORE
THE TINY PLUG-IN HEATER KEPT ME WARM
WHEN SUDDENLY — "BOOM!"

LOOKED DOWN – A GIANT LIGHT SPARKED NEAR MY FOOT
LIKE A HAND-HELD SPARKLER – SPARKS FLEW UPWARDS
SHOTS SPRAYED THE ENCLOSED AREA
WHITE SMOKE FLOATED UPWARDS

I STOOD INCHES AWAY FROM THIS EXPLOSION
MY PANTS OR I COULD HAVE GONE UP IN FLAMES!
PETRIFIED – HYPNOTIZED – MIXED WITH FEAR – A STATUE WAS I
SECOND PASSED – HUGE RELIEF, IT SUBSIDED – "WHAT JUST HAPPENED?"

THE WALL OUTLET — WAS WHITE — NOW SMUDGED WITH BLACK!
YET HEATER — STILL ON!
UNPLUGGED CULPRIT – WARMTH GONE – A PUZZLE INDEED
RESIDUE LINGERED FOR DAYS

FROZEN, LIKE AN ICE BLOCK WAS I – TWO DAYS, LATER
– ANOTHER MINOR BURST
BUILDING FALLING APART? – WIRING OLD?
UNPLUGGED EXTENSION CORD – LEADING TO THE OUTLET / SOCKET
EVER GRATEFUL, – AS A LATE CUSTOMER KEPT US OPEN...!

ELECTRICIAN – SOCKED IT TO ME
A NEW SOCKET, THAT IS!
WARMTH — IS NOW FOR THE ASKING

YET — LEERY AM I — GLAD — HOT WEATHER BEFORE US
AS I PLACID MY MIND TO EVERYDAY LIVING
AMAZING, WHAT WE TAKE FOR GRANTED — THE MIRACLE OF ELECTRICITY!

Reflection:

This poem is #51 – 'the one to grow on!' exceeding the 50 poems for each year in business (which happened coincidentally). Michael Day, a poet in our group, encouraged me to capture this incident. It's 'one' to learn from!

Facts:

Recommended electrician:
'David Hicks' = Kashina's husband.
Kashina worked for Jim for years, and now her teenage daughter, Cadence works @ Ming Quong, 'Perfect!'

THEIR LEGACY — LIVES ON...

TWO MENTORS — TWO FRIENDS
END OF 2019
ATTENDED TWO — 'CELEBRATIONS OF LIFE'
JERRY BALL — GARY BOGUE

THESE KIND-HEARTED SOULS HAD INTERTWINED
JERRY IN GARY'S COLUMN
WITH HAIKU
AND OFTEN-TIME- NEEDED ADVICE FOR THE READERS

GARY — VOLUNTEERED AT PARKMEAD ELEMENTARY
IN AWE, I ENJOYED THE INTERACTION

LASTLY — OUR POET'S GROUP'S
CHRISTMAS LUNCHEON
MEMORIES LINGER
THEIR LEGACY — LIVES ON...

— 11/11/2019

Facts:

Treat your senses to the Gary Bogue Trail — at the top of the peak, inhale deeply & enjoy the 365 degree view…also, both are authors — their books, the best. Jerry's books sold here @ MQ. For Gary's books — check with the Lindsey Museum in Walnut Creek.

Visit this website to discover the Gary Bogue Trail:

https://ridechronicles.com/tag/gary-bogue-trail/

My apologies for any employees omitted — but, know you are in my heart! ☺

Taylor, Mills Student
Corner of
Ming Quong Rd.
& Richards Rd.

**Ming Quong
Employees: Now ↑
& Then ↓**

Made in the USA
Columbia, SC
22 October 2020